HONDURAS & Other One-act Plays

Louis Phillips

Published by World Audience, Inc.
(www.worldaudience.org)
303 Park Avenue South, Suite 1440
New York, NY 10010-3657
Phone (646) 620-7406; Fax (646) 620-7406
info@worldaudience.org
ISBN 978-1-935444-38-1
©2011, Louis Phillips

ACKNOWLEDGMENTS

"Fog" was originally published in THE NASSAU REVIEW. *"Mindreaders"* was originally published in THE GEORGIA REVIEW. *"Life Guard"* was originally published by Prologue Press. *"Honduras"* was originally published in SANTA BARBARA REVIEW. *"Perilous Seas"* was winner of the John Curry Memorial Drama Prize (2010) and was published in CONFRONTATION. *"Fans"* was originally published in WORLD AUDIENCE. *"The Banquet"* was originally published in DRAMA & THEATRE. *"What I Did to the Great God of Comedy & What the Great God of Comedy Did to Me"* was originally published in CHIMERA CONNECTIONS.

TABLE OF CONTENTS

HONDURAS

A long stretch of white sand beach. CARROLL TROY, a very pale man of rotund proportions ENTERS. He is in his late forties and is dressed for a day at the beach. He carries with him a bright beach umbrella, a blanket, a radio, a paper-back book or two, a towel, a straw bag containing sun-tan lotion, binoculars, sunglasses, and whatever else he could possibly need. He wears flip-flops. He sets up his umbrella, spreads his blanket.

We hear the SOUND of the WAVES.

CARROLL: A day like this. What more can a man want form life? To be alive - with the sun beating down. Free from tensions. No worries, except maybe the worry of getting too much sun. (*Splashes sun-tan lotion over his ample frame*). Yes, sir. There is a lesson to be learned from this. But don't ask me what it is. I'm just going to stretch out on this beach and let life pass me by. What more do we want from life but that life pass us by, that the sun shine on us *(He unpacks his bag)*. Look at all this stuff! But not a newspaper, not one newspaper. Haven't read a newspaper in five days. The world can be going to hell in a hand basket, and I wouldn't know a thing about it. New governments all over the place, but the sea runs in and the sea runs out. Now that's philosophy. I really should have been a philosopher. No wonder Greece had all those great philosophers. It's because Greece has all those great beaches. You lie back on the white sand and you let the sun bronze your pores, and who couldn't think great thoughts?

He takes out Dialogues of Plato

CARROLL: Think of all the oceans and seas frozen over. What a sight that would be. It would play havoc with the tourist business, though. Imagine entire populations skating from one continent to another. But cold? God, it would be cold. I once read about a man who walked from Honduras to Russia. Walked right across the Bering Strait. Walked right across the frozen sea of language, ice crunching underfoot. I always meant to ask him why he did it. What would possess a man to walk all that way?

During the above, a YOUNG MAN in a PAGE-BOY'S UNIFORM has appeared on the beach. He is carrying a silver tray, a stack of telegram blanks, and a yellow pencil. He approaches CARROLL. Let's call the PAGE-BOY CORDOVA.

CORDOVA: Do you wish to send a telegram, mister?

CARROLL: What?

CORDOVA: Do you wish to send a telegram, mister?

CARROLL: Who? Me?

CORDOVA: There's no one else on this beach.

CARROLL: Who are you?

CORDOVA: I just want to know if you would like to send a telegram?

CARROLL: Do I look like a person who wants to send a telegram?

CORDOVA: It's possible.

CARROLL: No, it's not possible. So leave me alone. I came to the beach to be left alone.

CORDOVA: Very well.

CORDOVA starts away.

CARROLL: Wait! Do you work for the hotel?

CORDOVA returns.

CORDOVA: No, sir.

CARROLL: You're not one of the services provided by the hotel.

CORDOVA: I'm on my own.

CARROLL: What? You go up and down the beach soliciting telegrams from strangers?

CORDOVA: I merely ask if people want to send telegrams.

CARROLL: And people do?

CORDOVA: You'd be surprised.

CARROLL: I bet I would be. Come on! You can't make your living walking up and down a beach asking people if they want to send telegrams.

CORDOVA: I don't have to pay rent for a shop. No overhead.

CORDOVA: And then there are tips —

CARROLL: And then what do you do?

CORDOVA: When?

CARROLL: Well, suppose I decided to send a telegram. What would you do? You would take down my message and then what? Do you run over to the nearest Western Union shop? Or do you have a bicycle? Or motorcycle?

CORDOVA: No, I walk. It's not too far.

CARROLL: You're amazing kid. You really are. How old are you anyway? Eighteen? Nineteen?

CORDOVA: I'm old for my age.

CARROLL: And I'm tall for my height — Go on, get out of here. This is some kind of practical joke. Right? Some people at the hotel. For laughs? They sent you down here to annoy me.

CORDOVA: I didn't mean to annoy you, Sir. I thought you might have had a pressing message to get off your chest. Something that had to be said, and sent immediately.

CARROLL: What's wrong with the telephone? That's what I use the telephone for.

CORDOVA: A telegram has a long tradition to it. A history.

CARROLL: And telephones don't? Let me tell you something. Anything that lasts for more than five minutes in this world of ours takes on the status of a classic.

CORDOVA: A telegram provides a written record. And it speaks of class.

CARROLL: I don't believe this. The sun is shining. It's a hot summer day, and some yoyo dressed like Peter Pan comes up to me to ask if I want to send a telegram. What's the world coming to, I ask. It's a looney bin. I swear it.

CORDOVA: Please don't insult my uniform. I didn't insult your bathing suit.

CARROLL: What's wrong with my bathing suit?

CORDOVA: I'm sorry, Sir, but I can only talk with you if you are going to send a telegram. Otherwise, you are costing me valuable business.

CARROLL: Business? What business? People don't come to the beach to send telegrams.

CORDOVA: Very well, Sir. You're absolutely right – Good day.

CARROLL: All right! For laughs. I'll send a telegram. You're a novelty item, is that it? You really don't make your money sending telegrams. You make your money because you're a novelty. People get tired listening to the waves rushing in and the waves rushing out and the little fishes running about, and so they think: what the hell? Here I am on the beach, and I won't send a postcard home. I'll send a telegram. Tell me I'm right. You're a novelty item.

CORDOVA: Regard me any way you wish.

CARROLL: Do you take off your clothes?

CORDOVA: Well, sometimes it is a necessity. Before I shower, for example.

CARROLL: I mean are we talking strip-o-grams. Candy-grams? Singing Birthday Grams?

CORDOVA: Just tell me what you want to say – no singing, no dancing, no stripping – it's 25 cents a word.

CARROLL: What would I be charged if I walked over to the Western Union office myself?

CORDOVA: 10 cents a word.

CARROLL: Ah, so you are making a profit.

CORDOVA: It's a business like anything else. Of course you have to take into consideration wear and tear on the shoe leather.

CARROLL: You're barefoot.

CORDOVA: Well, if I were wearing shoes, you would have to take into account wear and tear on the leather.

CARROLL: If you were driving a Rolls-Royce, you could deduct depreciation on the engine.

CORDOVA: Now we're talking silly.

CARROLL: I didn't bring up the hypothetical shoes.

CORDOVA: Would you wear shoes on the beach?

CARROLL: Look, this is getting us nowhere. You want me to send a telegram and further your college education, and so I'm going to send a telegram. Then you'll leave me alone, you'll be happy, and I'll be happy, and the world will be just that much happier – what should I say?

CORDOVA: I don't think that's for me to decide. Is it?

CARROLL: What do people usually say?

CORDOVA: All telegrams that are sent through me are strictly confidential. I guarantee that no one will know what messages you send - just you, me, the telegrapher, and the person who gets the message at the other end.

CARROLL: Now I get it! What a racket.

CORDOVA: What's a racket?

CARROLL: How do I know that you'll even send the message? You'll walk away from here, your money in one hand, my message to the world in the other, and as soon as you're out of sight, spifftt – the message gets tossed away and you're off to the nearest bar.

CORDOVA: I don't drink.

CARROLL: And chickens don't have lips.

CORDOVA: And I don't throw the messages away. If you don't trust me, you can come with me yourself and watch the telegrapher at work.

CARROLL: If I do that I might as well do everything myself and save 15 cents a word.

CORDOVA: I provide a service – with a smile.
He smiles.

CARROLL: You're getting on my nerves.

CORDOVA: First you tell me to go away. Then you tell me to come back. Then you tell me to go away, then you call me back. Now you promise to send a telegram and still you don't come through.

CARROLL takes out a five dollar bill from his bag and gives it to CORDOVA.

CARROLL: All right. Here. Don't spend it all in one place.

CORDOVA: What's this for?

CARROLL: It's a tip. Five bucks. Take it. I'm a business man myself. I know how valuable time is. I didn't mean to waste your time.

CORDOVA: I'm sorry. I can't take this.

CARROLL: Yes, you can.

CORDOVA: I can only take a tip when I have provided a service.

CARROLL: You ruined my morning.

CORDOVA: A positive service. Are you certain you don't wish to send a telegram?

CARROLL: Positive.

CORDOVA: How about to your mother?

CARROLL: My mother is dead.

CORDOVA: I'm sorry, but perhaps you should send a telegram to let somebody know.

CARROLL: Let somebody know what?

CORDOVA: That your mother is dead.

CARROLL: She died over twenty-five years ago.

CORDOVA: There must be somebody who hasn't heard the news.

CARROLL: News? She wasn't exactly the queen of Egypt, buddy.

CORDOVA: It's not something you should keep to yourself.

CARROLL: Don't get worked up. Most people don't care about my mother one way or the other.

CORDOVA: Of course we care. You just have to give people a chance. The world is not as uncaring as you imagine.

CARROLL: I sell answering machines and vacuum cleaners.

CORDOVA: That has something to do with what I'm talking about?

CARROLL: Yes it does. I judge people on how they take care of their small appliances. If small appliances are any indication, our Earth is the most uncaring planet in the solar system, I've seen people do things to an electric toothbrush that the state wouldn't do to a convicted killer.

CORDOVA: I don't know anything about small appliances, but I know a lot about telegrams. Telegrams grab people where they live.

CARROLL: So do electric toothbrushes.

CORDOVA: Why don't we see if we can come up with a simple message for you to send?

CARROLL: The world is coming to an end. There are no free lunches. Wish you were here. Love, Carroll.

CORDOVA: Carol? Who's Carol?

CARROLL: That's my name. Carroll P. Davis of Akron, Ohio.

CORDOVA: I've been in the business a long time and I have never sent a telegram to or for a man named Carol.

CARROLL: Two R's. Two L's. What am I arguing with you for? If you don't like my name, take your business elsewhere. I can see that people are just clamoring to take advantage of your services. The line must stretch from here to Anchorage!

CORDOVA: I'm sorry

CARROLL: The customer's always right, buddy. That I can tell you. That's my family motto.

CORDOVA: You've given me such a hard time that I have violated the first rule of my profession.

CARROLL: Now it's a profession? You need a doctorate to do what do?

CORDOVA: I said I was sorry.

CARROLL: All right then. Tell me your name since I've told you mine. You're collecting names for a mailing list. That's it!

CORDOVA: Call me Cordova.

CARROLL: Call me Cordova. That's a line out of a spaghetti western.

CORDOVA: Of course it is. If it weren't for movies, half the people in the world would still be named for their grandparents. Now let me see if I have gotten your message correct. *The world is coming to an end. But the beach is nice. Wish you were here. Love, Carroll.* Two R's. Two L's. Sixteen words. Name is free.

CARROLL: That's not my message.

CORDOVA: Excuse me. I thought it was.

CARROLL: I was working off the top of my head.

CORDOVA: Most people do.

CARROLL: Not if they wish to succeed in the small appliance business.

CORDOVA: Tell me. There must be somebody back home you care deeply about.

CARROLL: Of course there are. A lot of people. My wife is back there right now taking care of the kids. That's why I was able to take this vacation, to get off by myself for the first time in fifteen years. I was the number-one salesman in my district, for answering machines, cordless phones, and toasters.

CORDOVA: Why don't you send a telegram to your wife that tells her how much you love her. You know. Those famous three little words. (*He writes on a blank*). I Love You.

CARROLL: That's only 75 cents. You can't get rich off a telegram like that.

CORDOVA: There's a two-dollar minimum.

CARROLL: I knew there was a catch to it someplace. But who would have suspected a cover charge on the beach?

CORDOVA: Let's send it.

CARROLL: Let me see it.

CARROLL takes the telegram blank and tears it in half. He lets the torn pieces fall to the sand.

CORDOVA: Why did you do that? That telegram was already to go.

CARROLL: Cordova, if that's your name –

CORDOVA: It is.

CARROLL: Do you know what would have happened if I sent that telegram? My wife would suspect that I'm having an affair with my secretary, that I was not down here on the beach all by myself, that such a telegram was prompted not by affection but by guilt. If men sent telegrams saying *I love you* to their wives, marriage as an institution would be out of business in a minute. No one could stand the strain. Obviously you are not married, or you would understand these things.

CORDOVA: I can't afford to get married.

CARROLL: I suggest you find another line of work.

CORDOVA: I'm very good at what I do. You just haven't had the opportunities to see me in action when the beach is crowded. Now do you want to help earn money toward my marriage or not?

CARROLL: I can't help you. I haven't composed a telegram since I congratulated my brother for being named Small Appliance Man of the Year.

CORDOVA: Your brother is a robot?

CARROLL: No. Actually, he's a member of the Kiwanis Club. He won that award from them nearly two decades ago – twenty years ago to you.

CORDOVA: Send him another telegram congratulating him for something else.

CARROLL: He hasn't done anything else. In twenty years he has gone from being a hot-shoe-salesman to becoming a bum. That's what life has been to him – a down-hill slide.

CORDOVA: Well, at least we're on the right track.

CARROLL: What track is that?

CORDOVA: Rule number two. Think of someone you want to send a message to.

CARROLL: Where are you getting these rules from?

CORDOVA: I've been in the business a long time. Whom do you wish to send a message to? Once you know that the words will tumble into place.

CARROLL: I can't think of anybody.

CORDOVA: A political party? A newspaper? A business corporation? The living, the dead, the yet unborn? The stars over your head?

CARROLL: Blood-suckers.

CORDOVA: The stars?

CARROLL: The whole lot of them.

CORDOVA: You're in a cheery mood.

CARROLL: I was. Now look -- the sun is going behind a cloud.

CORDOVA: It's only one small cloud.

CARROLL: I wandered lonely as a cloud.

CORDOVA: You could send poetry.

CARROLL: I'd rather hang by my thumbs.

CORDOVA: O.K. You give me no choice. If you wish to send a telegram, I'll violate my better business code of ethics. We'll work out a suitable message and then we'll draw a name and address at random from the phone book.

CARROLL: Run that by me again, Clyde.

CORDOVA: We'll send a message at random – and I'll give you a ten percent discount since your heart is not in it.

CARROLL: Are you trying to destroy me?

CORDOVA: I am trying to relieve your soul of the unbearable weight it is carrying.

CARROLL: If people back in Akron ever got wind that I was spending my vacation sending random telegrams to people I don't even know, you know what would happen to me? I'd be out of a job in a minute and I'd be committed to a loony bin.

CORDOVA: It has to be sent to somebody you know or to somebody you don't know. Most people fall into one of those two categories.

CARROLL: Or both.

CORDOVA: Here's your five dollars back – maybe I'll come back tomorrow. By tomorrow you may have something urgent to send.

CARROLL: I know what I want to say.

CORDOVA: What?

CARROLL: *(Runs toward the ocean, turns and yells)* Help!

CORDOVA: Help?

CARROLL: *(Runs back to CORDOVA)* That's right. Help.

CORDOVA: I see. And who do you want to send this to?

CARROLL: I'm not going to send it. You know why?

CORDOVA: Why?

CARROLL: Because I'm not going to spend $2.00 for a single word. Who do you think I am anyway? John D. Rockefeller?

CORDOVA: I'll be back tomorrow. In case you change your mind.

CARROLL: You do that. You come back every day of the week for all I care – I won't be here. I won't be here - do you hear me? I won't be here.

CORDOVA: Of course prices could go up by tomorrow. I do everything to hold my prices down, but I can't fight inflation. You shouldn't have torn up that page from my book. Paper costs money.

CARROLL: You should give your customers warning. No wonder you do such a lousy business. You don't give your customers enough warning.

CORDOVA: I told you I'd come back.

CARROLL: And I told you I won't be here.

CORDOVA: They all say that.

CARROLL: Why don't you take the hint?

CORDOVA: Where is there anywhere else to go? Please, lie down, enjoy your stay on the beach. Don't worry about me. I'll make a living somehow.

CARROLL: The sun has gone behind the clouds - see, didn't I tell you there was more than one cloud?

CORDOVA: Adios, Amigo.

CORDOVA turns and walks up the beach.

CARROLL: Don't *adios* me. Come back here. You've got me all worked up now - I've thought of somebody. *(He grabs his address book from his bag. Postcards fall to the sand)*. I've got aunts, uncles, nieces, nephews, cousins, friends – you don't think I don't have friends? My address book - see? *(He runs after CORDOVA. CORDOVA Stops)*. I have a whole list of names to choose from. I call them all the time. All the time.

CORDOVA: You thought of something to say?

CARROLL: Telegrams are for wimps, buddy – for English teachers – all that spelling.

CORDOVA continues off.

CARROLL: Even if I thought of something, I wouldn't tell you –

HE returns to his blanket, sits down, picks up his book. He opens it.

CARROLL: I'm going to complain to the Chamber of Commerce – that's what I'm going to do – write them a letter. Give them a call. That's what I'm going to do. Send them a telegram – (he closes the book). This isn't good beach reading. Too heavy. That's the trouble with me. My eyes are always bigger than my stomach. Always think I'm going to do so much – I really should have brought a newspaper they sell in supermarkets. Something simple. Something with recipes and horoscopes. Something with headlines like: *Unwed Mother, aged 10, gives birth to a vacuum cleaner* – (looks at his watch). *I was taken for a ride in a UFO.* Now those are people with real stories to tell – well, at least I know I'm not going to stay here any longer.

A BEAUTIFUL TANNED WOMAN in the briefest of bikinis enters.

CARROLL: I'm not going to give that idiot another chance to ruin my morning. (He packs his gear). There are always people invading your privacy, wanting to know more than they are entitled to know – trying to sell you things, even on a beach. Planes flying back and forth with banners. Eat at Joe's. Messages galore. Messages over our heads even.

The WOMAN starts to put down her towel.

CARROLL: Don't sit here!

Startled. She turns towards CARROLL. With a certain haughtiness, she pushes her sunglasses toward the tip of her nose and stares murder at him.

CARROLL: I don't mean to be rude, but I'm trying to tell you what's going to happen. You'll be lying there on your towel and this guy dressed in a weird costume is going to come up to you and ask if you have any urgent messages you want to send – and

17

then where will you'll be, sister, huh? Where will you be?

She replaces her sunglasses. Ignoring CARROLL, she stretches out on the beach.

CARROLL: Well, don't say I didn't warn you. I gave you plenty of warning. I hope you're thinking of something to say. Otherwise it's going to ruin your whole morning –

CARROLL starts off.

CARROLL: Something new. Something soul-shattering. Something different. Something original. Otherwise it's going to ruin your whole morning – I'm telling you – I'm warning you!

The WOMAN raises herself, makes certain CARROLL has left. She TURNS ON her RADIO. We hear strains of VALENCIA.

LIGHTS OUT. CURTAIN.

LIFEGUARD

The Players

PAMELA (Sharon)

ACHERON ROONEY

CALVIN JOYCE

SHARON (Pamela)

MAN WITH CIGAR (can be played by actor who plays Calvin Joyce)

ANOTHER MAN (can be played by actor who plays Acheron Rooney)

The Place

At rise we are confronted by a gigantic lifeguard stand that occupies stage center and which dwarfs anyone who stands beside it. At first the light upon the stand and the beach is somewhat overwhelming for the sun has risen from the summer ocean and hovers over the beach with a maniac eye.

Seated upon the lifeguard stand is Acheron Rooney. A muscular young man of about twenty-five years of age dressed in a solid dark blue bathing suit and a white undershirt. His skin is bronzed from the sun and his blonde hair is bleached and sandy. He whistles to himself as he covers his arms and long legs with coconut tanning lotion.

As Acheron is engrossed in his tanning ritual, Pamela enters. She is sixteen years old or so, and exudes, paradoxically, worldliness and innocence in her stance and walk. Dressed in a white bikini, she is nearly as tanned as Acheron himself. She removes her sunglasses and leans provocatively beside the stand, her fingers instinctively seeking out patches of white paint which she begins to strip from the peeling and weathered wood. She chews gum and from time to time will stretch it forth from her mouth and snap it or allow it to momentarily cling to her deep red lips.

We can hear the surf and the gulls.

PAMELA: Another stupid boring rotten monotonous existentialist day, with the sun shining its boring rotten monotonous existentialist eye over the entire beach.

ACHERON (*hardly interested*): Sharon?

PAMELA: No, Pamela. I'm the one who's knocked up. Remember?

ACHERON: When it comes to sperm, out-of-sight, out-of-mind.

PAMELA: Yeah, well Sharon wants you to come up to the house for lunch this afternoon.

ACHERON (checking feet): Is that an invitation or a command?

PAMELA: We've got you scheduled for the lunch-hour shift. Otherwise, you'll have to stand in line with the rest of the studs.

ACHERON: The surf is pretty rough today. I've got to put up my "Beware of Man of War" signs, my "Beware of Jellyfish" signs, my "Be Careful of the Undertow" signs, my "Look Out for the Eels and Sand Sharks, my "Be Careful not to Touch the Electric Eels" signs, my "Don't swim in the Red Tide" signs, my....

PAMELA: Some crummy beach, huh… I don't know why everybody's so hipped up about private beaches either.

ACHERON: Public beaches have to have lifeguards.

PAMELA: I'd rather have jellyfish myself.

ACHERON: Tell your sister thanks for the invitation, but I brought my lunch. (*Indicates a brown bag*). Tuna fish and sprouts.

PAMELA (*makes a face*): Tuna fish and sprouts….yuck.

ACHERON: What's wrong with tuna fish and sprouts?

PAMELA: Look, pansy, if you want to sit up there on your ass all day and explore variations that go into the making of tuna fish realities that's up to you. However, my sister says that if you come up for lunch, we'll all take off our bathing suits and sit around naked like we did yesterday, before you violated me in your typical Trojan manner...you're a real ape, that's what you are. Your fundamental core of authentic being is all screwed up.

ACHERON: You and your twin sister think you own the world, but you're both so young you don't know which end is up.

PAMELA: That didn't bother you yesterday, did it?

ACHERON: I didn't bring a tuna fish and sprouts yesterday.

PAMELA: Sleep with the tuna fish sandwich then...You're a real throw-back, you know that, Acheron? Your mother must have hated you to name you Acheron.

ACHERON: My mother doesn't hate me!

PAMELA: A real momma's boy, huh...I knew it all along. You don't know what to do with real red-blooded American women. That's why you're afraid to come up to the house.

ACHERON: I have a job to do. I have to keep people from drowning!

PAMELA (looks at the water): There's nobody in the water. Look at it. Nobody's going to go in on a day like this.

ACHERON: They might. They might.

PAMELA: They might drop out of the sky also but that doesn't mean you have to stand around twenty-four hours a day holding out a safety net. Suppose you do swim out there and save somebody's life, what then? The Chinese say that you have to be responsible for that person for the rest of that person's life. Now that's yucky. That's worse than marriage. At least in marriage you can get a divorce. But if you save somebody's life, there's no way you can escape the implications of that. You'll wear that responsibility around your neck like that whistle for the rest of your perverted days. You'll wake up sweating at night, with nightmares. And don't hand me any of that reverence of life stuff because that went out with the bomb...I know all about you lifeguards. You just want to be somebody's big, blue-eyed hero. Lifting some gorgeous woman out of the sea so you can apply mouth-to-mouth resuscitation. You can't wait until somebody drowns so you can plop your fat tongue into her mouth.

ACHERON: We don't put our tongues into their mouths.

PAMELA: Lifeguard, hah! You're into necrophilia.

ACHERON: Pamela. Go home before your tongue gets sunstroke.

PAMELA: It was Sharon's idea, not mine. She always swoons for real yucky pocked-marked acne-ridden creeps. But that's her problem, right? What do you care about my sister's problems? She could drop dead at your smelly feet for all you care. If people die in their beds, that's no concern of yours. It's only if they're swimming in the ocean and they're attacked by stomach cramps or sharks that you begin to sit up and take notice. But my own twin sister's up at the house eating her heart out over your coconut oil bawd and you don't give a damn.

Toward the conclusion of Pamela's soliloquy, Mr. Calvin Joyce enters. He is a middle-aged man who stares forlornly at the sea. Dressed in an olive-gray trench coat, he carries an old inner tube with him and a bicycle pump. With his brown stocking cap pulled tightly about his forehead. Calvin sits down and empties a bucket of sand from one of his shoes.

ACHERON: Bye, Pamela.

PAMELA: You better eat your tuna fish sandwich before it hears the call and returns to the sea.

ACHERON: Why don't you come back when the tide is in? Say when it's all the way up to your ears.

PAMELA (*to Calvin*): You'd better not expose yourself to me, mister. (*Exiting*). Dumb beach. You can't come down here anymore without some creep exposing himself...Those perverts think just because it moves, we're supposed to salute it.

Calvin remains impassive to the charges. Instead he goes about his business. Acheron looks at him with amused curiosity. Calvin is now engaged in the business of adding air to his inner tube. Acheron climbs down from his tower and crosses toward Calvin. By now the brightness of the scene has faded. The sky has become dark and overcast. Wind blows scraps of lunch papers across the beach. There is the rumbling of thunder in the distance.

ACHERON: I hope you don't think you're going in swimming on a day like this. The surf's way too rough. I'm keeping everybody out today. Christ, look at all those sharks out there. You'd think they'd have nothing to do than swim back and forth, back and forth. Life should have a purpose. It shouldn't just be back and forth like the sharks or the waves.

No responses from Calvin.

ACHERON: Hey, mister, you hear me? You can't go in today. Too dangerous. You hear the thunder? Soon there will be lightning. The ocean's the most dangerous place in the world to be in a lightning storm.

CALVIN: When do you go to lunch? Isn't it about time for you to knock off for lunch?

ACHERON: Huh?

CALVIN: Shouldn't you go to lunch?

ACHERON: I bring a tuna fish sandwich for the first time in weeks and all of a sudden everybody's worked up about my going out to lunch. What's it to you, Mac? What do you care if I starve to death or not?

CALVIN: I didn't mean anything. I'm just blowing up my inner tube.

ACHERON: Don't bother. I'm not letting anybody in the water today.

CALVIN: Can I blow up my inner tube anyway? Or do I have to have a purpose in mind?

ACHERON: Don't ask me about such things.

CALVIN: Sile et philosophus esto…Hold your tongue and you shall pass as a philosopher.

ACHERON: Hmmmmm?

23

CALVIN: Something my Latin teacher would say a lot.

ACHERON: That's a dead language for you. I like living things myself. Now look at the sea out there. Now that's alive. Real choppers. I've seen waves fifteen, twenty feet high, and they'll make your heart leap with excitement. (*He crosses back to the stand*). There's nothing like the sea in all its wildness to give a man a sense of the vastness and mysteriousness of life. (*Climbs back to his post*). So what's the sense of learning dead languages when you can come out here and look at the sea all day, and think of all the life that's going on underneath the surface – did you ever think how many people would drown every day if there weren't lifeguards around to look after things?

Calvin, carrying his inner tube crosses to the lifeguard stand.

CALVIN: Is it all right if I ask you a question?

ACHERON: Sure, why not? It's a public beach. Lifeguards all along here. If I can't answer your question, maybe there's somebody else who can.

CALVIN: I was just wondering how much you get paid to keep people from drowning.

ACHERON: What?

CALVIN: I figure you probably don't make very much, right?

ACHERON: Right. But there are a lot of other satisfactions involved. You can't afford to overlook all the other satisfactions. *He gazes back towards the house of Pamela and Sharon, and sighs.*

CALVIN: Why don't you take this two hundred dollars here and go off and have some lunch. You see these are Traveler's Checks, so they're good. You'll have no trouble cashing them. It's just like money they say. I'll just endorse them and so you can fill your own name in. Or, I'll write it in. What is your name?....

ACHERON: Two hundred dollars for lunch?

CALVIN: Three hundred.

ACHERON: What are you up to, Mister?

CALVIN: I'm not up to anything.

ACHERON: Oh yes you are. To come down to the beach on a day like this, lugging an inner tube under your arm and offering me three hundred dollars out of nowhere. What do you think I have for lunch? I'm a very simple man. I've never spent three hundred dollars for lunch in my whole life.

CALVIN: Can I tell you the truth?

ACHERON: If it's the best you can do. I prefer fantasy myself. I like to sit up here and stare out at the sea and pretend beautiful women are going to fall madly in love with me and that some refugee from a Latin school is going to come out of nowhere and hand me three hundred dollars for lunch.

CALVIN: You can have more than three hundred dollars. I don't care. Take all my Traveler's Checks. Take my watch. Take the bicycle pump. Just go away for a while.

ACHERON: So that's it. You want me out of the way. Not ever having studied Latin, I may be a little slow, but I catch on eventually.

CALVIN: You can have my shoes. Hand-sewn from Montevideo – from a cousin of mine who teaches Latin at the university there.

ACHERON: I don't want your inner tube. I don't want your Traveler's Checks. And I certainly don't want your bicycle pump. Just let me alone so I can do my job.

CALVIN: I want to be left alone, too.

ACHERON: But I was here first. You're the one who's got to leave me alone.

CALVIN: I'm going to leave you alone. As soon as you go off to lunch, I'm going to swim out to the ocean and drown myself...If my inner tube floats back to shore, you can have that too.

ACHERON *(stunned)*: Let me get this straight. You want to swim out in the ocean and drown myself.

CALVIN: I guess that's the only way to do it, isn't it?...I mean if I want to drown myself, I guess I'll have to go out there.

ACHERON (*angry*): Why are you telling me this? If you want to drown yourself, go ahead and drown yourself. But wait until I go off duty. Come back in the dead of night for all I care. But what are you telling me for.

CALVIN: Don't you understand? I don't want to wait. I can't wait any longer. Every moment of living is torture to me. It's now or never. So why don't you go away for an hour or so. Even lifeguards must take breaks.

ACHERON: I brought my lunch today.

CALVIN: Throw it away.

ACHERON: There are people starving in the world, and you want me to throw my lunch away.

CALVIN: Then give it to me and I'll eat it.

ACHERON: No. You don't want to go in the water on a full stomach.

CALVIN: That's exactly what I want to do. I want to get cramps and drown…Give it to me.

ACHERON: No. You're not going into the water, and I'm not going to let you drown. If you had come here yesterday at this time, I would have been up at that house up there, having the time of my life with two young nymphos, and then you could have gone down for the third time and nobody would notice, except maybe God and a couple of jellyfish. But that was yesterday, and today is today, and today I'm here.

CALVIN: I don't want to drown myself yesterday. I want to drown myself today, right now, right this instance. Look, if you want to sit there and eat your tuna fish sandwich, it's all right with me. Just promise me, cross your heart and hope to die you won't make any attempt to rescue me. Even if I scream. Even if I panic at the last second, no matter how loud I scream and yell for help, you just sit there with my watch and stuff and don't make any attempt to rescue me. Don't pay any attention to me at all.

ACHERON: I can't do that.

26

CALVIN: Why not?

ACHERON: It's against the rules for one thing. And it's a blot on my record for another. I can't have people drowning on my beach while I'm on duty. They'll take my Red Cross card away from me. They'll strip me of my swimming trunks, take my tanning lotion and my radio. Look, Mac, I don't want to face the music…I may not be my brother's keeper, but that doesn't mean I'm going to sit back and watch him drown.

CALVIN: Suppose I leave a note? That's what I'll do for you. I'll leave a suicide note telling the whole world that I drowned of my own choosing and that it wasn't your fault after all. No negligence on your part whatsoever. It's my fault because I told you not to rescue me. Do you have any notebook paper? I didn't bring any notebook paper with me. It's very hard to plan for every contingency.

ACHERON: If you really wanted to drown yourself, you wouldn't have brought along an inner tube. You're just like everybody else. You just want some attention. That's all.

CALVIN: I can't swim.

ACHERON: That's what I mean. Not being able to swim shouldn't be a handicap if you want to drown.

CALVIN: I have to go out over my head, don't I?

CALVIN PUTS ON HIS INNER TUBE. HE STILL HAS HIS SHOES AND SOCKS ON.

ACHERON: Not necessarily. You can drown in your bathtub if you try hard enough.

CALVIN: I don't want to drown in two feet of water. It'll make me look like the village idiot.…Perhaps I could write a note on the back of one of my Traveler's Checks?

ACHERON: You can write *War and Peace* on the top of a pin head for all I care, but I'm not going to let you drown.

CALVIN: You're a rotten human being. Your fundamental core of authentic being is all messed up…It's my life. I can do what I want

27

with it.

ACHERON: I'm responsible for what happens on this part of the beach.

CALVIN: I suppose you think you own the water, too.

ACHERON: I don't own the water. I'm just patrolling it. If you want to drown, go somewhere else. Perhaps there's a lifeguard somewhere who doesn't take life seriously. Maybe there's a lifeguard somewhere who doesn't care about his safety record.

CALVIN: I'd be better off dead.

ACHERON: Not if you can afford two hundred dollars for lunch.

Calvin has made a dash for the water, an awkward flopping run, further hampered by the bulk of the inner tube.

ACHERON: Help you...Come back here, you creep.

Acheron blows his silver whistle, scampers down the sand, and rushes off-stage. We can hear shouts and cries. A few moments later, Acheron re-emerges, lugging Calvin upon his shoulders. Calvin, still clutching to his inner tube, is covered with wet sand. He spits out a mouthful of salt water.

CALVIN: Put me down.

ACHERON: You try a stunt like that again and you're going to be in trouble. I'll call the police and have them cart you off to the loony bin.

CALVIN: I didn't break any law!

Acheron sets Calvin down on the sand.

ACHERON: Look, schmuck, it's against the law to kill yourself... and don't say anything, because ignorance of the law is no excuse.

CALVIN: That law ought to be revoked.

ACHERON: The people who want it revoked aren't around to vote on it.

CALVIN: It doesn't make sense. Nothing in life makes sense.

ACHERON: That's the first thing you've said today that makes a lot of sense. (*Tosses Calvin a towel*). Here, wipe yourself off before you get pneumonia. Good thing I tackled you before you threw yourself all the way in or you would really be a mess.

CALVIN: Look at me. I'm all wet. I'm covered with sand.

ACHERON: So what? You're going to kill yourself anyway.

CALVIN: I want to go out with style.

ACHERON: There's no style with an inner tube, schmuck.

CALVIN: My name's Calvin. Calvin Joyce.

ACHERON: Calvin Joyce. I guess that's reason enough to kill yourself.

CALVIN: What's your name?

ACHERON: Look, I don't want to know your stupid name. I don't want any human contact with you whatsoever. To me you're nothing but a cipher. A dead zero. A zilch.

CALVIN: I'm a zero, a cipher, and a zilch, and you wonder why I want to kill myself.

ACHERON: I want to kill myself too. Everybody wants to kill themselves. That's what life is about.

CALVIN: But you don't really mean it.

ACHERON: And neither do you. You're a jerk, Calvin, that's what you are. You come down here simply because you want some attention. Well, I'm not going to give you any more attention. It's obvious to me you're a failure, and I'm not interested in failures. I'm interested only in success, the people on top, read me? I'm communicating with you on a very human level. Failures are like jellyfish. They lie along the beach waiting for somebody to step on them and get stung.

CALVIN (*pause*): Thanks. I needed that.

ACHERON: You needed what?

CALVIN: It clarifies my view of myself. I'm a complete and utter failure. I can't even drown myself.

ACHERON: Let go of the inner tube, Calvin. Without your inner tube maybe you'll sink to the bottom like a rock.

CALVIN: You won't let me near the water.

ACHERON: Drowning is a terrible way to go. Did you ever think that as you're going down for the third time that your entire life is going to flash before your eyes, and then you're really going to be depressed. That's no way to go. You don't want to leave this world in a depressed state...

CALVIN: But I am depressed. Nobody loves me.

ACHERON: Of course they do. Even I love you.

CALVIN: You do?

ACHERON: Yeah, now go home and stick your head in the oven and leave me alone.

CALVIN: I don't have a home. I don't have an oven. I don't have anything.

ACHERON: I don't want to hear it. You know why I'm a lifeguard? Because I like to listen to the waves, that's why. The waves rolling in and the waves rolling out. That's something you can count on and it's soothing. Go ahead, I'm waiting. Quote some more Latin at me. Reach into that dead heart of yours and bring forth some dead phrases from some dead language.

CALVIN: My parents died in a plane crash...(*No response from Acheron*)...My daughter is living with a drug addict...(*No response from Acheron*)...My house burned to the ground last week. (*No response from Acheron*)... Day after the insurance policy expired....I forgot to send the premium in. My son has contracted venereal disease and is going insane...(*No response from Acheron*)... do you hear me?

ACHERON: I hear you, mister....

CALVIN: Calvin....and I drink all the time. And I'm impotent.

ACHERON: Impotent, huh?

CALVIN: You don't have to rub it in.

ACHERON: I'm not rubbing it in. I'm simply repeating what

you're telling me!

CALVIN: You didn't have to pick that to repeat. You could have repeated anything else I said!

That's the trouble with this world. As soon as a guy is down, people can't wait to trample all over him.

ACHERON: I tell you what, mister...

CALVIN: Calvin....

ACHERON: I'm going to do you a favor. Back up there are the hottest pair of identical twin sisters you've ever met in your life. I'll take you up there and introduce you and they'll cure your troubles just like that (*snaps his fingers*).

CALVIN: It won't help. Nothing will help. What good is it to revel in the flesh when everything is so transitory? As my Latin teacher would say...

ACHERON: I don't want to hear about your rotten Latin teacher.

CALVIN: You want to know what else? I just found out today that all my credit cards have been stolen...there's somebody out there in that jungle, running up bills, charging everything in sight to my name. If I lived past today, I'd be the highest credit risk in the United States.

ACHERON: Cut it out, mister, you're breaking my heart.

CALVIN: I'm not mister. Can't you call me by my name? Is that too much trouble?

ACHERON: Your name sucks. You suck. This whole rotten day sucks. Now I've heard enough. Go ahead, kill yourself. You've convinced me. Because you're a jellyfish, that's what you are. Except if I stepped on you, you wouldn't even splat. What you've experienced is nothing. Not a drop in the ocean of misery. For chrissakes, just look around you. The whole goddamn world is drying up. It's like standing in the middle of the ocean and watching it turn to desert. I mean people are dying on the streets in India, starving to death in Africa.

CALVIN: You really know how to cheer a guy up.

ACHERON: Schmuck, I wasn't trying to cheer you up. I'm trying to make you see the facts of life. That's not the ocean out there; it's a million miles of human tears.

CALVIN: But you're right. I'm depressed about the human situation, too. It's not just myself that I care about. No, I'm worried about the whole world too, and I don't see a future for anyone.

ACHERON: Then follow through with firm resolve. Make posthaste. I'm calling your bluff because you public suicides are all alike. You just want a little attention. But I don't have any for jellyfish. So go ahead. There's the ocean out there waiting to hug you with its cold wet arms.

CALVIN (*staring at the ocean*): That's very poetic....Cold wet arms.

ACHERON: Poetic?...(*Holds up his weight-lifting magazine*)...I got it off an advertisement for a deodorant...Now I'm giving you ten minutes to drown yourself or I'm calling the cops...and that means loony-tunes for you, baby.

CALVIN: You mean it? You really mean it? You're going to let me drown myself?

ACHERON: Go swipe an egg from the bluebird of happiness and stuff your head into Davy Jones' locker. You can scream your head off to your heart's content and I won't hear a thing.

CALVIN: What about your safety record?

ACHERON: Jellyfish don't count. Only men and women. Real men and women. Even if you wash up on the beach, nobody will notice you.

CALVIN: You don't care about me at all, do you?

ACHERON: That's right. You win the grand prize.

CALVIN: I tell you everything about myself, and you don't blink an eye. No, all you care about are the starving millions in Africa, because you don't have to see those. You don't really have to worry about them, but if somebody's right in front of you.....

ACHERON: There's nobody in front of me. The Invisible

32

Schmuck.

CALVIN: That's not nice.

ACHERON: Aaugh.

CALVIN: You could show some concern. After all I did offer you three hundred dollars. Not many people had given you three hundred dollars in life.

ACHERON: It wasn't cash.

CALVIN: Traveler's Checks are as good as cash.

ACHERON: Nothing is as good as cash.

CALVIN: I'll take the checks back then.

ACHERON: Go ahead. Maybe they'll give you extra weight and help drag you to the bottom.

CALVIN: I'm going...!

ACHERON: Bon voyage.

CALVIN (*hurt*): You're not going to come after me?

ACHERON: I'm on my lunch hour now. I'm not here.

Calvin, taking his inner tube, goes off. There's a pause. The sound of waves. Calvin returns.

CALVIN: Maybe you ought to swim out and pretend to try and save me...You know...just to make it look good....In case somebody's watching.

ACHERON: I'm going off duty. (He *begins setting out his "Lifeguard is OFF Duty. Swim at own risk." sign*) Drown on your own time, buster.

CALVIN: I was just thinking of you, that's all. I mean I don't want you to get into trouble. Even in suicide, I'm fundamentally unselfish.

ACHERON: Thanks, but nobody's watching. Nobody will come near the beach on a day like this...Too many sharks. Look at the sharks out there. Now if you want my considered opinion, you won't get the chance to drown. The sharks will eat you alive before

33

you get halfway out.

CALVIN: Look at them all. I didn't even see them before.

ACHERON: Don't let them bother you though.

CALVIN: A man wants to do a simple thing and it becomes so complicated. Lifeguards, inner tubes, sharks, low tide, lousy weather...it's a miracle anybody gets to drown at all.

ACHERON: Come on, Calvin. I'll take you up to Pamela and Sharon. They'll straighten all your problems out.

CALVIN: You finally remember my name?

ACHERON: It's embroidered on your bathing trunks.

CALVIN: Yeah. That's right. My daughter did that before she ran off with a junkie.

ACHERON: Put your coat on.

CALVIN: Oh no...I see through you...I see what you're trying to do. All that stuff about the sharks and everything else. You're just trying to talk me out of the only significant act a person can perform...I'll show you. I'll show everyone. You're all going to miss me after I'm gone...

ACHERON: You're facing the wrong direction. The water's that way.

CALVIN: Yeah, that's right. I just got turned around, that's all....Eyes look your last...delenda est Carthago!

Calvin dashes toward the sea. Stops. Turns to make certain that Acheron isn't following him, and then continues his lemming-like journey. Acheron stands quietly by the lifeguard stand, watching and waiting. We hear the sound of a giant splash.

ACHERON: Christ! He's going through it....sharks and everything.

Acheron picks up his weight-lifting magazine and leafs through it. As he does so, Sharon enters. She is indeed Pamela's identical twin sister. Only the color and style of the bathing suit have been changed.

SHARON: All right you creep. Pamela's told me about you

34

standing us up for a tuna fish sandwich. After all we did for, with, and to you yesterday.

ACHERON: Didn't I have enough trouble with your sister this morning?

SHARON: Double your flavor, double your fun.

ACHERON: Come one, Sharon, I have a lot of work to do. I have signs to set out.

SHARON: Yeah, you really look busy, drooling over the men with the weights....Pamela said you were in a lousy mood, but what can you expect from...(*Looking out at the ocean*)...Hey, who is that creep out there in the water? Look at him. He must be crazy to go out there on a day like this...

ACHERON: There's nobody out there.

SHARON: He's flailing his hands like he's in trouble.

ACHERON (*not interested*): You're imagining things.

SHARON: There's somebody drowning out there. I can see him. Look!

We hear the distant cries of Calvin hollering for help.

SHARON: He's crying for help.

ACHERON: Look, Sharon. That dumb ass out there wants to drown, so just forget about him.

SHARON: What do you mean, forget about him?

ACHERON: It's all right. We have the whole thing worked out. It isn't even going to appear on my record.

SHARON: He's going under. Don't just stand there. Do something!

ACHERON: Didn't you hear what I said? He wants to drown.

SHARON (*frantic*): Then why is he calling for help?

ACHERON: That's what people usually call when they're drowning. What do you want him to shout? The Gettysburg Address?

SHARON: Acheron, do something. Please!

ACERHON: He doesn't want me to.

SHARON: If you're not going in after him, I am.

ACHERON: Oh no you're not! This is my section of the beach. If a man wants to drown here and if I give him permission, then you have to stay out of it.

SHARON: Take your sweaty hands off me....Pamela is right, Acheron. You talk a big game, but when the chips are down...

ACHERON (interrupting): I promised I wouldn't save him. You want me to break a sacred bond between one human being and another?

SHARON: Is that a whale swallowing him?

ACHERON: That's his inner tube.

SHARON: Do I have to do your work for you?

ACHERON: There are sharks out there, honey?

SHARON: So that's it. You're handing me all this metaphysical crap when all it really boils down to its sharks...(To Calvin)...Hang on, I'm coming.

Sharon dashes to the water. We hear a great splash.

ACHERON: Sharon, don't....I'm warning you....You're disobeying a lifeguard...Oh Christ, look at her. She doesn't know the first thing about saving lives, so why does she have to play Sheena, Girl of the Jungle, all of a sudden...

We hear Sharon's voice: "Help me. I have a cramp."

ACHERON: That water must be freezing...(*Takes down a can of shark repellent and sprays himself*)...I'm not going in there without putting shark repellant on...It's one thing to let the loony drown, but I have to save Sharon...Hold on! I'm coming!

Acheron dashes for the water. We hear a great splash. There is a pause. There is the sound of Calvin's voice. "Help me, for God's sake." From the direction of the beach house, Pamela enters. She carries a bright orange lawn chair and a portable radio playing music.

36

PAMELA (*setting up her chair*): Look at them out there. Who would have thought that they would be crazy enough to go swimming on a day like this...The water is yucky and everything.

Sound of Acheron's voice in the distance: "Oh my God, a shark has got my foot."

PAMELA: Those jokers. Sharon and Acheron are always fooling around.

Sound of Sharon's voice: "Pamela help me!"

PAMELA: Look at them, hanging onto each other, rubbing bodies in the water...Those two never know when to quit...And look at that other creep out there...What's he doing?...Oh good God, he's really drowning...They're all in trouble...Sharon!...Acheron! Oh my God, I have to do something! Why isn't there anybody around?

Pamela sheds her robe and runs toward the water. Calvin's voice: "I'm going down for the third time!"

PAMELA: I'm coming! Don't panic! You mustn't ever panic!

We hear the sound of a great splash as Pamela enters the water. A pause. A man with a cigar enters, dressed in a terry cloth beach robe. He wears sunglasses and has a blue towel draped about his neck.

MAN WITH CIGAR: Perfect day for the beach. It's not littered with bodies from one end to the other.

Pamela's voice: "Over here, over here!"

Acheron's voice: "The sharks. The sharks."

MAN WITH CIGAR: Oh for God's sake. What's going on out there?

Sharon's voice: "Help us. We're drowning!"

MAN WITH CIGAR: All those people out there are in trouble. Look at them. (Begins undressing). I can't save them all, but perhaps I can save one...Why in hell isn't there a lifeguard on this beach when you need one?...Don't panic! I'm coming. Just try to stay afloat.

There is the sound of another great splash. As the light begins to dim, another man makes his appearance upon the beach. As he begins to realize what is going on and gets prepared to carry out another rescue mission, the lights go out, leaving Pamela's radio playing forlornly on the beach.

CURTAIN.

FOG

The stage is bare. Only patches of fog are visible. Out of the fog emerge two persons — a stylishly dressed woman and the curator of the museum, a man in a sports jacket and slacks. The woman, aged 23, is Connie Graham. The man, slender, mustached, bespectacled, is Jonathan Lee. Connie opens a guide book to the museum. Jonathan indicates the fog.

JONATHAN: Here it is.

CONNIE: It is?

JONATHAN: It is.

CONNIE: Yes. But what is it?

JONATHAN: Fog.

CONNIE: Yes, but what is it exactly?

JONATHAN: It's all explained for you in the Guide Book.

CONNIE: I was hoping you would tell me. I can read the book anytime.

JONATHAN: Fog occurs when minute particles of ice or water are suspended in the atmosphere near the Earth's surface, restricting horizontal visibility to less than one kilometer.

CONNIE: That clears it up.

JONATHAN

If it clears it up, it's not fog.

SHE LOOKS AT HIM:

JONATHAN: Sorry. The last person I showed the museum to was eight years old.

CONNIE: Is this the only place in the world we can see it?

JONATHAN: As far as I know. You are privileged to be in the World's Only Museum of Fog. I doubt if any other museum would be foolish enough to follow my lead.

CONNIE: I came all the way from Naples to see it.

JONATHAN: You've picked a particularly uncrowded day.

CONNIE: I suppose it's not much of a tourist attraction.

JONATHAN: We do the best we can, but, of course, it is impossible to compete with the video arcades.

HE INDICATES A BENCH, THEY SIT.

JONATHAN: In Cuernavaca, under the shadow of the volcano Popacatepetl, there is the Museum of Mist. Have you been there?

CONNIE: I have been everywhere.

JONATHAN: Have you stood trembling upon the lips of Saturn?

CONNIE: I have.

JONATHAN: Have you gloried in the delicate dramas on Phobos and Demos?

CONNIE: I told you that I've been everywhere.

JONATHAN: Very well. I no longer doubt you.

CONNIE: (*Smiles*) The Museum of Fog was the only place left to see.

JONATHAN: We are unique

CONNIE: No doubt.

JONATHAN: In Tokyo, there is the Snow Museum.

CONNIE: I know.

JONATHAN: In Buenos Aires, the Museum of Thunder and Lightning.

CONNIE: Lightning frightens me. I am glad to be rid of it.

JONATHAN: I fear you have picked the least interesting of all the Museums. All we have is Fog, though with a little luck, we can in the next room conjure up a fog bow.

HE INDICATES THE NEXT ROOM. CONNIE SHAKES HER HEAD.

CONNIE: I am in no rush to move on.

SHE REMOVES THE COLORFUL SCARF FROM HER HEAD AND SHAKES OUT HER BLONDE HAIR.

CONNIE: Are you?

JONATHAN: No, you're the first visitor I've had in weeks. Not counting the eight year olds, of course. She enjoyed my little jokes though. Downstairs we have walls covered with photographs of fog...mountains shrouded in fog, meadows covered with fogs, night scenes...and, then, every once in awhile, when I get desperate and feel the need to perk up interest, we sponsor a Fog Film Festival. English mysteries mostly.

CONNIE: Really?

JONATHAN: No. Not really.

CONNIE: I'm not eight years old anymore.

JONATHAN: Sorry.

CONNIE: There's no need to apologize. Why do you always feel the need to apologize?

JONATHAN: I don't...Look, there's a cafeteria across the street. That is, if you're hungry.

CONNIE: I'm not, thank you. I really don't have much time.

JONATHAN: Well, our exhibit is not very extensive. We're still in the process of setting in exhibits. Driving through fog might bring the younger people up.

CONNIE: Really?

JONATHAN: Perhaps. We are very serious in our pursuits. The study of Fog is a serious subject. It doesn't attract the fly-by-night personality, if you know what I mean.

CONNIE: Fly-by-night?

JONATHAN: Whatever. Tell me, how did you find us?

CONNIE: I was in Naples when one of your brochures dropped into my hands. It is well-written. I particularly liked the quotations from the poets. It must have taken you a long time to track them down.

JONATHAN: There was no rush. I could have spent the rest of my life writing it. Isn't it somebody's Law that Work Expands to Fill the Available Time?

CONNIE: Are you a writer?

JONATHAN: No. I collect fog. I hold it in my hands and then it disappears.

CONNIE: That's all you do?

JONATHAN: It's not enough?

CONNIE: I'm sure it keeps you busy.

JONATHAN: Not busy enough. But I used to have ambitions. I worked all the time. From sunrise to sunset. For years I pursued a long and boring book about a man nobody ever heard of, but then I realized the world is filled to overflowing with human beings that nobody has ever heard about, even now as I speak, even now as we spill over onto the stars and other planets taking our small confusions and large prejudices with us.

CONNIE: Is the book in print?

JONATHAN: Oh no. It never even got that far. I erased it right off the disk. Now I have switched to Dante and I revel in passages where sinners struggle through the fog to God, a fog of their own making, I might add.

CONNIE: You don't have the true scientific temperament?

JONATHAN: We start off in one direction and we end up in another. I have always been a slow learner, and I have always been interested in subjects that other people were not interested in...And you?

CONNIE: And me?

JONATHAN: Are you here on holiday?

CONNIE: Yes and no. My editor assigns me out-of-the-way stories and I do the best I can.

JONATHAN: I do the best I can too.

CONNIE: The Museum of fog seemed like a worthy addition to the Teletextual Funnies.

JONATHAN: You're a reporter?

CONNIE: Not really. My husband…actually my ex-husband…owns the company. But I have to do something.

JONATHAN: Why?

CONNIE: Why, what?

JONATHAN: Why do we have to do anything?

CONNIE: It keeps us amused, I suppose.

JONATHAN: Too much unwanted, unneeded labor. Millions of human satellites wandering about in a daze. But now we have everything under control. Even the vicissitudes of the weather.

CONNIE: Tell me about the different kinds of fog.

JONATHAN: Mental fog? Spiritual fog? Phineas Fog?

CONNIE: I was hoping for something more scientific.

JONATHAN: I'm afraid that is as scientific as I get.

CONNIE: Not a good recommendation to run a museum of science.

JONATHAN: Scientists get bad press. We get blamed for all the evils, but, if push comes to shove, and it usually does, I can always claim that this is not a museum of science. This museum is more mystical than that. You can hold the fog in your hands; you can stumble through it like a blind man, holding onto the shoulder of the guide in front of you, and still not know what it is.

CONNIE: These subscribers to Tele-text demand facts. We are no longer soothed by fictions.

JONATHAN CROSSES TO A SPEAKER AND PRESSES A BRIGHT RED BUTTON ON A POST.

JONATHAN: Well, if it's facts you want, you merely press this red button here. Our museum is dotted with pre-recorded tapes. We can give you facts until you cry out for relief.

A VOICE COMES OVER THE SPEAKER. WE HEAR THE OPENING WORDS TO ALEXANDER McAIDES' Fog.

SPEAKER: Every fog is a cloud, only it is a cloud that rests upon earth. Conversely every cloud is a fog only it is lifted by rising air and shaped by losing energy, chiefly caused by the winds. The matter of gaining or losing heat is all important. It makes or unmakes cloud and fogs. Fog may indeed be regarded as the parent or original source of all cloudiness..."

JONATHAN STOPS THE SPEAKER.

JONATHAN: Did you get all that?

CONNIE: About clouds and fog being one and the same?...Some of it.

JONATHAN: No matter. You can go back and listen to your heart's content. The tape automatically goes back to the beginning.

HE PRESSES THE BUTTON. WE GET THE START OF THE SPEECH AGAIN.

SPEAKER: "Every fog is a cloud, only it is a cloud that rests upon earth..."

JONATHAN STOPS THE SPEAKER.

JONATHAN: And so on and so forth.

CONNIE: And so on and so forth.

JONATHAN: Of course one of the main concerns of people on our planet...aviators especially...used to be the modification of fog. We have many scientific pamphlets dealing with that issue. Every once in awhile we have guest speakers in. Sometime next month I believe we have some academic type lecturing on The Terminal Velocity of Fall for Water Droplets in Stagnant Air." Not very exciting, I fear, but we do what we can to keep an understanding of fog alive. We're in the process of developing a program for children.

CONNIE: When I was eight years old, I remember reading a story about an old man who was living in the mountains. He was driving home late at night and he missed a turn in the road. He missed it because the author said the road was covered with a blanket of fog. I remember reading that phrase over and over again, and I couldn't figure out what kind of blanket that would be. I didn't really understand what fog was. I mean I had access to the definition of it. We had the definition but we didn't have the thing itself.

JONATHAN: That is one of the wonders of modern life. We have definitions, but we don't have the things themselves.

CONNIE: But thanks to you and your museum, I now understand the thing itself. I finally see what caused the man to drive off the road…He went over the cliff and died. I think.

JONATHAN: Maybe it wasn't the fog at all.

CONNIE: What wasn't the fog?

JONATHAN: The reason he drove over the cliff. Cause and effect are often more complicated than they seem, even to the unscientific mind. Perhaps he drove the car over the cliff because he didn't want to live anymore.

CONNIE: I think he had a lot to live for. Wife. Family. Good job.

JONATHAN: The reason might not have been outside the car. It might have been within the steering mechanism itself. Or computer error. Computer error covers a multitude of sins.

CONNIE: A computer had nothing to do with it. This is an ancient story.

JONATHAN: A true story?

CONNIE: A fiction.

JONATHAN: Fiction. Most persons don't use that word anymore…

CONNIE: I'm not most people.

JONATHAN: No, you're not. Tell me, you journeyed all this way, not to do a story on my little museum, but to understand some story? A fiction?

CONNIE: I will write something for my editor. I have to keep busy.

JONATHAN: A long and roundabout journey for a woman who has been everywhere.

CONNIE: You forget. This woman has never journeyed through fog, at least not the kind of fog that would drive a person to his death.

JONATHAN: But the fog you find here is not the kind of a fog a driver might encounter upon the road, or a filer in the air, or a ship upon the high seas. The fog we have here is out of context. And don't forget fog is not always a killing fog. Fog has been known to save lives too. Washington was able to slip past the British ships on New York's East River, and hence, because of fog, the course of the entire American Revolution was changed.

CONNIE: Are you married?

JONATHAN: Excuse me?

CONNIE: I merely inquired whether you were married or not?

JONATHAN: No. Unattached. I float through the world unattached…Are you going to put that in your story?

CONNIE: What?

JONATHAN: That the director of the Museum of Fog is unattached? Human interest. Isn't that what they used to call it?

CONNIE: I never know what I'm going to do until I do it.

JONATHAN: Put in lots of fog. It's good for atmosphere.

CONNIE: I didn't mean to offend you.

JONATHAN: I don't like to live this way, but there are not that many options opened to us.

CONNIE: I should have thought there were too many options opened to us.

JONATHAN: Perhaps. Perhaps that is why I choose to stay inside surrounded by my fog…But no. I'm not married. I was once. Doesn't everybody have someone once?…And you? Your ex-husband, you said?

CONNIE: We've separated. But then what does marriage mean anymore? Not much, I'm afraid.

JONATHAN: Any children involved?

CONNIE: No, thank God. We had seven boys, but, of course, none measured up to the high standards set by the IPS, and so they were quickly terminated.

JONATHAN: Interplanetary specifications get higher every day they say.

CONNIE: Oh, they're not that high really. It's just that we all some from such inferior stock.

JONATHAN: Earthlings try harder.

CONNIE: Too hard if you ask me.

JONATHAN: But all seven?

CONNIE: Extra-uterine, but even so…

JONATHAN: Even so. There won't be much left to the next generation if the IPS keeps that up.

CONNIE: It's what the governing council wants, isn't it?

JONATHAN: I don't know. I'm not privy to their innermost counsels.

CONNIE: Artificial weather. Artificial intelligence. Artificial births.

JONATHAN: It's certainly not easy to know what to want.

CONNIE: At least you have your museum to fall back upon. I have only make-shift work, granted to me because my husband…ex-husband…owns the company.

JONATHAN: I am merely regulated to the most innocuous Museum that the IPS can foist upon a lost soul.

CONNIE: Humanoids can do it better.

JONATHAN: Of course humanoids can do my job better. That's what dawned upon me. I worked hard at the beginning of my life, worked very hard, until it came upon me in a bolt of lightning that hard work meant nothing. Absolutely nothing. Why there are some men who awake in the artificial dawn and gold falls from the sky into their laps. What was all the effort for them?

CONNIE: I have tapped a bitter vein.

JONATHAN: Of course I haven't lost seven children to the IPS, so I don't know that depth of feeling...

CONNIE BURSTS INTO TEARS.

JONATHAN: I didn't mean to....

CONNIE: No...It's not you.

JONATHAN: I'm sorry.

CONNIE: There you are. Apologizing again.

JONATHAN: Take my handkerchief.

CONNIE: I've been crying a lot lately. I can't help myself.

JONATHAN: It's the fog. It puts everybody into a melancholy mood...Besides I had no right to inquire about your children.

CONNIE: Rights?...Beggars can't be choosers. Oh well, I shall not ladle you any more soup from the tureen of self-pity.

JONATHAN: I take it you haven't been separated long?

CONNIE: No. Not long!

JONATHAN: I've been through it myself.

CONNIE: Of course. Who hasn't. We have controls on everything but our personal lives. They are the real weather.

JONATHAN: She had deep blue eyes. I could have drowned in those eyes. Perhaps I did.

CONNIE: What happened?

JONATHAN: Nothing happened. Nothing ever happened.

CONNIE: Sometimes things happen.

JONATHAN: And then you turn around and they are not there anymore.

CONNIE: Your wife had blue eyes?

JONATHAN: No. Not my wife. My wife claimed I was sucking her dry. I guess I was. All I wanted to do was to finish my book about something nobody cared about, and my selfishness drove her insane. She was reading the article about solar eclipses, looked at a picture of the eclipse of the sun in a magazine and she went blind.

CONNIE: From a picture?

JONATHAN: Well of course, there was no physical basis for the blindness. Went to all the specialists. Psychiatrists. The whole works. But nothing could clear. She didn't want to see...

CONNIE: Didn't want to see what?

JONATHAN: That I didn't love her any more. That I couldn't. That everything in my life had gone sour. That I was wandering without a sense of direction. Without purpose...But because I was married, the girl with the blue eyes was afraid. All the IPS enactments against adultery, you know. The New Age of Moral Uprightness or whatever the catch phrase of the day were. We would have long lovely terrifying meetings, but she wouldn't sleep with me. We were like planets or brilliant satellites whirling about each other. And, of course, I couldn't leave my wife. She had gone blind. And I kept wondering what picture would I stare at that would deprive me of my eyesight. And now that I am free, unattached, floating through the world, the woman with the blue eyes has married someone else.

CONNIE: You're still in love with her?

JONATHAN: I don't know. You become what you look upon, says Dante, what you give your attention to. And I looked upon her so long...And you? You still in love with your husband?

CONNIE: No. I hate him. He sucked me dry too...I want to see him dead....

JONATHAN: No, you don't.

CONNIE: Oh, but I do. Is that terrible of me?

JONATHAN: Wrath is terrible. In Purgatory, on the Cornice of the Wrathful, the sinners are enveloped in a cloud of thick black smoke. They stumble through the fog listening to the voices of the meek and the mild.

CONNIE: The meek and the mild. How quaint.

JONATHAN: A Dantean judgment. Not mine. Nothing is mine.

CONNIE: If you ask me, there is too much meekness in the world.

JONATHAN: The meek shall inherit the Earth.

CONNIE: Of course we will. Once the people in power get through with it, the Earth won't be worth inheriting.

JONATHAN: Attacks on the IPS will not be tolerated. You can be turned in for seditious talk.

CONNIE: So can you.

JONATHAN: I hope I shall be exiled to some small cozy satellite where people know what they want, where they climb up the mountains of self-doubt to stand in the sunlight of God's Grace.

CONNIE: God's Grace. That really is backward looking when the Interplanetary Committees give us things so much more practical. Museums of weather for example, so that us poor humble folk can receive a taste of the past.

JONATHAN: Well, running a museum where no one comes is not a particularly graceful state.

CONNIE: Nor is loving people who don't love back...I hate being abandoned. With all my soul. That is if I have a soul left.

JONATHAN: Abandoned? As a child?

CONNIE: As a wife. Or whatever you call it when your husband leaves you for someone else.

JONATHAN: Your husband has left you for a younger woman?

CONNIE: Younger? Let's just say he left me for *another* woman.

JONATHAN: Another. Yes, that is better than younger.

CONNIE: Who knows if it's better. It's just different.

JONATHAN: You can invoke the Married Powers Acts.

CONNIE: Of course I can. I can have him strung up by his testicles and I shall. After all, I'm not like you. I no longer believe in States of Grace. I no longer care if there is a God or not. Or some mysterious power shaping our destinies.

JONATHAN: Then what do you care about?

CONNIE: The longer I live the less I know what to care about...I care about the pain I feel...The pain that is gnawing at me and won't go away.

JONATHAN: The Angel of Meekness calls to us and we know not what to answer, except that we answer with our pain, which proves, more or less, that we are alive and breathing, more or less.

JONATHAN: A warning to ships struggling through fog.

CONNIE: It sounds haunting.

JONATHAN: When such a bell is operated by water, the sound is very irregular. Sounds that haunt us should come in on a more steady pulse...

CONNIE: Cloche de Brume. I haven't heard a French phrase in decades.

JONATHAN: Of course there are many different ways of fog signaling...At least there were, in the days of multiple languages...There are sounds transmitted through the air; there are sounds transmitted through the water. And then there are fog signals transmitted by radio waves. All included, for no extra charge, in our guided tour.

CONNIE: More than one way of calling for help, you mean.

JONATHAN: More than one way of answering. Though, of course, it is more poetic, more Dantean, if you will, to believe that there are Angels on the shore, fluttering their wings to create waves to push us away from the rocks.

THE SOUND OF A GONG IS HEARD. THE GONG IS IN ANOTHER ROOM OF THE MUSEUM.

JONATHAN: Sifflet de brume...B-R-U-M-E.

CONNIE: I can spell it, thank you.

JONATHAN: I'm sorry. I forget that you are no longer eight years old and have been everywhere.

CONNIE: Why do you keep throwing that in my face all the time?

JONATHAN: Perhaps for the same reason that you keep reminding me how apologetic I am.

CONNIE: Well, you are.

JONATHAN: Well, maybe I have a lot to apologize for. You don't know.

CONNIE BEGINS TO LAUGH.

JONATHAN: What's so funny? Did I say something funny?

CONNIE: What's so funny is that we have just met and yet we're beginning to sound like an old married couple.

JONATHAN: I guess we are. I'm sorry.

CONNIE: Please.

JONATHAN: Let me show you some of the exhibits in progress. We have some wonderfully informative tapes. Slide shows.

CONNIE: I have a better idea. Why don't you close up and walk me back to my hotel. I have lots of champagne back in my room.

JONATHAN: Champagne?

CONNIE: Another of the forbidden joys. My friends smuggled me two bottles because, no doubt, now that my husband has abandoned me, they think I should become an alcoholic.

JONATHAN: It is a generous offer, but...

CONNIE: Becoming numb might be my only comfort.

WE HEAR THE SOUND OF THE FOG BELL. JONATHAN CROSSES TO A SPEAKER MOUNTED UNDER A

PHOTOGRAPH OF A SHIP SURROUNDED BY FOG. HE PRESSES A BUTTON, WE HEAR THE TAPE.

SPEAKER A:

"When atmospheric conditions, and more particularly fog, make lighthouses, light vessels, and visible marks as aids to navigation more or less difficult to distinguish, then sound or radio signals are employed for the purpose of distinguishing points along the coast and making them recognizable.

"These signals are generally given at lighthouses or light vessels themselves, by certain buoys, beacons, etc. in their immediate vicinity."

CONNIE CROSSES AND TURNS OFF THE TAPE.

CONNIE: Are you deliberately ignoring my invitation?

JONATHAN: I'm….

CONNIE: Sorry. I know. God, I hate being this needy…Look at me! Do I have grief written all over me?

JONATHAN: No. Of course not….

CONNIE: *(Mimicking him)* Of course not.

JONATHAN: You're very beautiful.

CONNIE: But not beautiful enough it seems.

JONATHAN: Believe me, I'm flattered by your invitation. I really am…

CONNIE: It's against the law. Is that what you're afraid of?

JONATHAN: I'm afraid of a lot of things.

CONNIE: I'm afraid of being alone. That's what I'm afraid of. I'm in a strange city. You're the only person here I've even talked to.

JONATHAN: Naples must have been more lively.

CONNIE: Lively? Oh yes, I suppose I could have stood out on a street corner with a sign around my neck. *Getting Any?* Desperate woman looking for a man…

53

JONATHAN: There is no reason for you to see yourself in such a desperate light.

CONNIE: Oh no. No reason at all.

JONATHAN: Please don't be angry with me.

CONNIE: I'm sorry...You see. You've got me doing it.

JONATHAN: (*Indicates his museum*) You see this is the city in which I live.

CONNIE: And you never venture out.

JONATHAN: And I never venture out.

CONNIE: Not even for champagne?...Or whatever?

JONATHAN: Not even for champagne...or whatever. You see when my first wife left me, the image I had was of someone taking a razor to me, cutting me open, pulling back the skin, and exposing all the nerve-endings for all the world to see. I don't ever want to be that exposed again.

CONNIE: To your fog then. Yes that is what I shall drink to.

JONATHAN: If we could only go back in time.

CONNIE: Yes, with all the inventions that the IPS has forced upon as, you would think they could do that for us...

CONNIE BEGINS GATHERING TOGETHER HER THINGS.

JONATHAN: To a time before they took away the weather. We would grope our way back to a city completely covered by fog, a fog so thick that you can't see your hand in front of your face....The ships are moored in the harbor. They can't move. Nothing moves. The fog bell is ringing. And there are sirens. But nothing moves upon the streets. Figures may be glimpsed every once in a while. They are seen, and they vanish. Like ghosts. We could wander through a city where everything has come to a halt because of the thickness that clouds our vision. And voices call to us. Voices cry out to us. But the voices that call are not the voices of angels. They are not even the voices of terrified human beings. They are voices without bodies. Where am I going? Who will

54

show me the way? For days, for months, for years the fog never lifts. The fog bell rings and rings, and we look for the sun in vain. We wonder if the sky over our heads has been taken from us. And all the time our eyes are searching for something that says yes, yes, yes. Something that grants us permission to live.

CONNIE: I wasn't asking you for your permission to live, thank you.

JONATHAN: I'm so glad. It's not in my power to grant it.

CONNIE: When I was very young…I must have been six or so, I saw my father naked for the first time. He had stepped out of the bathroom, and I saw him and I ran to him, and he put up his arms and pushed me away…As if he were angry with me. Angry with me for something I didn't understand. Later I did. His embarrassment, or his momentary confusion. But by then it was too late. The damage had been done.

JONATHAN: We do damage and then we undo damage. We do damage and then we undo it. It keeps us occupied.

CONNIE: Here, there, and everywhere.

JONATHAN: Will you be going back to Naples?

CONNIE: I don't know. I already have been there.

JONATHAN:

"Luogo e la giu da Belzebu remoto tanto quanto la tomba sis distende, che non per vista, ma per suono e noto d'un ruscelletto che quivi discende per la buca d' un sasso, ch' elli ha roso, col corso ch'elli avvolge, e poco pende. Lo duca e io per quell cammino ascoso intrammo a ritornar nel chiaro mondo…"

CONNIE: You certainly are a repository of dead and dying languages.

JONATHAN: Old words searching for new meanings.

CONNIE: Old women searching for new experiences.

JONATHAN: "Down there is a place distant from Beelzebub as far as the cave extends, a place known, not by sight, but by sound, the sound of a small stream winding through a rocky tunnel. The way down slopes slightly. My guide and I followed the dark path in order to return to the world of light."

CONNIE: Thank you, Mr. Broome, for the translation.

JONATHAN: Once I gave up on my book, a book which no one would read, I decided to dedicate my work to moving thoughts from the old languages to the new.

CONNIE: For which generations, yet unborn, shall thank you...Good-bye.

JONATHAN: Wait, I haven't told you my funny story about the drivers in the fog who followed each other home.

CONNIE: You forget. I am not amused by funny stories.

JONATHAN: I remember. You are not eight years old anymore, no longer reader stories of people going astray...Please, allow me to accompany you to the door.

CONNIE: That won't be necessary. I have been shown the door once too often. Ta-da. Be sure to look for my story in the tele-texual funnies. I am certain it will be of great amusement to you.

SHE EXITS. JONATHAN CROSSES BACK TO HIS EXHIBITS. HE PRESSES THE RED BUTTON. AS THE TAPE BEGINS, THE FOG IN THE MUSEUM INCREASES.

SPEAKER B:

In New York City on March 14, 15, 16 1929, we can find a good example of fog and high dust content. "The fog which prevailed on these three days and especially the last was one of the densest that had occurred in twenty years. It was very dense over the water. All transatlantic lines had to anchor in the harbor, and even ferry service was, if not entirely suspended, run in such a manner as to greatly incommodate passenger." (*A. McAdie*)

WE HEAR THE FOG BELL RING.

LIGHTS OUT. CURTAIN.

MIND READERS

The Time: *The Night of April 20, 1967*
The Place: *The basement of a theater in Athens*

The stage should be completely bare, with the exception of two very elegant and expensive red velvet chairs. Seated in one chair is Henry Vaughan Vanderhorst who performs under the name Manzini. He is, in fact, one half of the world famous mind-reading act - The Great Manzinis.

Manzini, as he is known, is dressed in a tuxedo and is in the process of taking off his black shoes, exchanging them for something more comfortable, his old slippers that have travelled the world with him and his wife. Manzini is a tall, solid man, with a goatee and a head of white hair. Over his left eye he wears a white patch. In fact, he is the epitome of the magician/mind-reader.

Standing behind the second chair is a stylishly dressed, slender young woman in her late twenties. She is Ms Helena Michaelides, a reporter for one of several conservative daily newspapers. She is also the hostess of a morning talk show on radio. She has put on her eye-glasses to study some notes she had taken on a note-pad.

HELENA: A very distinguished audience, don't you think?

MANZINI: *(Not without humor)* Any audience that the Great Manzinis appear before become distinguished by the very presence of the Great Manzinis.

HELENA: Ah, but King Constantine himself...How rare for him to take an evening in public these days...He was impressed.

MANZINI: Was he?

HELENA: Yes, I could tell...Your wife and yourself had us all amazed.

MANZINI: But Kings are easily impressed, aren't they?

HELENA: Not Greek kings.

MANZINI: Any king. The ordinary world is a marvel when you are trained to live so far above it.

HELENA: I don't believe that Constantine is far above the ordinary, do you?

MANZINI: My wife's relatives say he is not very well educated.

HELENA: When one is king in a time like this education comes in many forms.

MANZINI: Not the least of which is reading the newspapers. Every day, Greece is in trouble. Greece is on the edge of anarchy. One never knows whether the papers report the news or create it.

He crosses to a stand that holds a bucket of champagne. He removes a bottle, studies it.

MANZINI: Of course, Thea says you are a remarkable writer. She really enjoyed your stories about the student uprisings in Thessaloniki...

HELENA: I am fortunate. I am allowed to cover many different kinds of stories.

MANZINI: Yes, from ASPIDA to mind-reading in a few easy lessons...

HELENA: Do you read Greek?

MANZINI: My wife reads Greek. I do not. This is her country. All her family, friends, and relatives are here...Whereas mine...Well, mine are scattered to the four winds. You will share some of this champagne with me, no? It is a gift from Major Arnoutis...Everyone has been quite generous with their gifts.

HELENA: *(laughing)* Beware the Greeks bearing gifts...

MANZINI: Well, I know that story.

HELENA: Just a sip...I still have my work to do.

MANZINI: I still have my work to do too.
He hands her a full glass.

HELENA: And what is that?

MANZINI: To get you drunk and to seduce you. You certainly must have realized that.

HELENA: Your reputation has preceded you.

MANZINI: Has it?

HELENA: I shall keep up my guard.

MANZINI: That is always a good procedure. To keep up one' guard...*(Raise his glass)* To freedom.

HELENA: To freedom.

MANZINI: I always enjoy it when Thea brings me to her country. There are so many countries where there are so little freedoms.

HELENA: Wherever we are, our thoughts are always free.

MANZINI: As long as there are not too many people who can read minds.

HELENA: Like Thea?

MANZINI: Like Thea.

HELENA: Since you admire Democracy so much, have you ever given thought to living here?

MANZINI: I have given...or have been given thought about everything. Haven't you?

Helena laughs.

HELENA: I don't know. How can I possibly know what I have never thought about?

MANZINI: We think therefore we are. Is that it?

HELENA: That's what they say at the University.

MANZINI: Well, I know another way.

HELENA: Another way of what?

MANZINI: Of becoming aware of all the subjects that we have never thought about. Life tells us.

HELENA: Are we back to journalism again? You mean *Life* magazine tells us what we have never thought about? Or *Epokhes*?

MANZINI: Not the life of the written word, but the other kind of life. It tells you what you have never thought about by presenting you with who you are. With what we become.

He has used these lines before. He studies Ms. Michaelides to see if they have had any effect upon her.

MANZINI: I remember when I was a young man at the University...

HELENA: What University?

MANZINI: It doesn't matter.

HELENA: To me it does. To my readers.

MANZINI: No.

HELENA: There are great gaps in your biography.

MANZINI: That's exactly what I am trying to say, Miss Michaelides. It is the gaps that make us interesting. The ignorance.

HELENA: And what did you remember?

MANZINI: I remembered that I had a friend who had thrown a few rocks, had broken some windows...It was a demonstration against the government...the fascists had come to power...and an old professor of mine...A man who had secured tenure by remaining silent all his life, who would go every which way the wind blows....He had called me aside and said I had been lying...And indeed I had...I had told the University authorities some lies to protect my friend...to keep him out of jail...And the old professor was being very philosophical, or perhaps he was just afraid, since so many people make a political philosophy out of fear...He asked me directly, I remember, "How can you of all people, Mr. Vaughan, put friendship before Truth." It did seem a kind of dishonor, especially to a young Idealist like myself, to give Truth second-best...until a few months later a phrase came to me, perhaps it was from another mind, that Friendship itself is a truth. Wouldn't you agree?

HELENA: Yes, I think I would.

MANZINI: It was like any remark one things of too late. And so I walked all over Berlin, trying to track the Professor for he had left the University...But he had disappeared. It was as if he had never existed except to chastise me. And then, later in my studies, I stumbled across a quote that I have always carried with me. "I hope I never have to choose, but if I have to choose between betraying my country and betraying my friend, I hope God grants me strength to betray my country."

HELENA: I think it is a perfectly horrible thing to say.

MANZINI: Do you?

HELENA: Yes, but may I quote you.

MANZINI: No, I told it wasn't mine.

HELENA: So much the better.

MANZINI: Besides it makes me sound pretentious. *(He makes his little joke)*. "Manzini, you are pretentious!"..."Pretentious, *Moi?*"

Helena laughs.

MANZINI: But how many thoughts in this world can we really call our own?...Have more Champagne...

HELENA: You really are trying to get me drunk.

MANZINI: I am not very often left alone with such an attractive woman. And if I have to work fast, it is because my wife and I are not staying in Athens very long...

HELENA: Where do you go from here?

MANZINI: My wife wants us to be in Thessaloniki on the 28th to help Papandreou launch his campaign...Give some moral support as it were, since he is an old friend of Thea's family...and from there, we do have some fairly substantial bookings.

HELENA: I would imagine that mind-readers would be very valuable in government, don't you?

MANZINI: As what? Court jesters?

HELENA: No, as spies, I think it would be very handy for people to know what their enemies are thinking.

MANZINI: Women do make good spies…Mata Hari and all that, but I doubt if spying would be a profession that Thea would be attracted to. Of course what is there to spy on in Greece? Merely communist plots hatching under every bush, uniforms stashed away into every locker. That is, if one can believe the right-wing papers. Though of course there is one great advantage to serving whoever is in power. The kind of prestige that one doesn't get from the wicked stage. Thea's gifts would be given their full due. We wouldn't have to change ourselves into Bozo the clown to make a living. Because that is what happens you know. You are given a great gift - whether it is painting or writing or dancing - and you have to turn yourself into a clown in order to survive. Why. I have seen the greatest actors of my generation engaged in selling toilet tissue and automobiles.

HELENA: You don't enjoy being on the stage?

MANZINI: I can't say that, can I? Not when Thea and I climbed out of the automobile wreck into show business history. Or a small portion of it, anyway. Though show business history seems much more perishable than any other kind.

HELENA: Entertaining millions of people is no small feat.

MANZINI: True, but mind-reading has very little to do with entertaining. It should be a statement, a witness to what we could become if…if we could harness these marvelous and untapped powers. After all, when people make love, the mind is the best sex organ in the world, isn't it?

HELENA: (Smiles) Are you asking me?

MANZINI: When it comes to theories about sex I always try to turn to a beautiful young woman for corroboration.

HELENA: I am afraid I am not that young.

MANZINI: It is all relative, isn't it?

HELENA: But you can trust me. It's all a trick, isn't it?

MANZINI: What? Sex?

HELENA: No. Mind-reading.

62

MANZINI: After what you saw tonight, before such a prestigious audience? Why even the poets turned out. But, of course, why shouldn't the poets be interested in the life of the mind. We have one of George Themeis' book around this dressing room somewhere. My wife won't go anywhere without a trunk filled with books. You think we were carrying the local library with us from town to town. But of course so many towns even have libraries anymore. As if great segments of the population have chosen to grow up ignorant.

HELENA: Please, don't change the subject. I know what I saw out there tonight.

MANZINI: That's right. You saw Bozo the Clown. The oldest act in existence. The Great Manzinis. A woman is seated upon a stage, on a bright red velvet chair, and she is blindfolded by a devilishly handsome man….namely me…who then wanders out into the audience, holds up objects, and the woman calls out the names correctly. Once of the Generals held up one of his good luck charms…Thea names it, and even King Constantine is astonished. A remarkable performance. And of course, I am ashamed of it, because the Great Manzinis are capable of so much more. But then who isn't? What isn't? Greece herself is capable of doing so much better.

HELENA: Well, we applaud the presentation, the subtitles of the code…

MANZINI: No code!

HELENA: Whatever you want to call it. The wonderful display of memory.

MANZINI: No memory.

HELENA: But to call it mind-reading.

MANZINI: *(Finishing the sentence)* Is it fraud.

HELENA: Confess. You can trust me.

MANZINI: Certainly I can trust you. Anything I tell you will be written up in one of the Vlachou's newspapers, or broadcast to the world on your morning radio show...What is it called?

HELENA: *All About Athens.*

MANZINI: A modest title. You need more of the spirit of exaggeration in you. All true Greeks love exaggeration. The simplest argument turns into a life and death struggle.

HELENA: To a Greek there is no such thing as a simple statement.

MANZINI: True. But even I love to enlarge the truth. Thea and I are The Great Manzinis. Not the *Good* Manzinis. Nor even the *fair* Manzinis. And why limit yourself to Athens? Is Athens the whole world?

HELENA: To some people it is.

MANZINI: Yes, to some people it is.

HELENA: I inherited the title of the radio show from somebody who died.

MANZINI: Isn't that the way. So many of our thoughts are taken from people who have died...Pretentious, *Moi?*... By the way, you can come closer. I am not going to make a pass at you.

HELENA: What are you talking about?

MANZINI: You are standing there thinking what you will do if I make a pass at you.

HELENA: I am not!

MANZINI: Oh but you are. The way you stand there allowing your forefinger to rub around and around the top of the champagne glass...It's a certain give-away among certain types of women.

HELENA: Oh, it's just a nervous habit. I have seen men do it also.

MANZINI: Of course, if you and I made love it would not be an unpleasant experience.

HELENA: Please. May we talk about something else?

64

MANZINI: Certainly, I have no desire to make Tom jealous.

HELENA: Tom?

MANZINI: Private pilot for Colonel Makarezos.

HELENA: Who told you about Tom?

MANZINI: You did.

HELENA: I did not.

MANZINI: Ten minutes ago you were thinking whether you should call Tom or not. So many thoughts are merely flying around waiting to be picked up by sensitive...or should we just say receptive minds.

HELENA: Does your wife know that you carry on like this?

MANZINI: Carrying on? This isn't carrying on, my dear. Carrying on comes later.

HELENA: My husband wouldn't approve.

MANZINI: You're not married.

HELENA: Because I'm not wearing a ring?

MANZINI: Rings don't mean anything.

HELENA: Obviously not.

MANZINI: My wife encourages my flirtations. They keep me young.

HELENA: I don't believe that.

MANZINI: I guess I don't look young enough.

HELENA: I don't believe that your wife approves of your flirting with me.

MANZINI: You can ask her yourself. Whenever she returns from being wined and dined by the rich and famous...

HELENA: Why didn't you go with her?

MANZINI: I thought that being alone with you would be rich with possibilities.

HELENA: I'm afraid I won't be able to stay much longer. I want to type this interview up before I go to bed...

MANZINI: I am at the mercy of the press then...Here, allow me to make amends for my bad behavior...*(He removes a deck of cards from his jacket pocket)*...Here, take a card....
Manzini holds out the deck of cards. Helena selects one.

MANZINI: You have my word of honor, whatever that's worth, that it's an ordinary deck.

HELENA: The Three of Hearts.

MANZINI: *(Disappointed)* You weren't suppose to tell me.

HELENA: Please! I don't have to be entertained by card-tricks.

MANZINI: Very well, then. Just think of a card. I'll do it the hard way.

HELENA: The Nine of Clubs.

MANZINI: Once again, you weren't suppose to tell me.

HELENA: Sorry. But I thought that if you were going to read my mind, we could skip all the hocus-pocus and get right to it.

MANZINI: I hope you don't feel the same way about sex.

HELENA: You always return to the same subject.

MANZINI: Perhaps when you reach my age. No, that is not fair. Age has nothing to do with it. It is only your beautiful presence that inspires me.

HELENA: It is the champagne talking. Not you.

MANZINI: Champagne never has any effect upon me. But making love. There is a subject of universal interest. Is it not? The sexual energies, wave-lengths if you like, when a man and a woman are alone together in a room...It is just another form of mind-reading, is it not?

HELENA: Is it?

MANZINI: Please, I am a very simple man. If you answer my questions with questions, I shall soon grow very confused.

HELENA: I am sorry, but why do I get the feeling that every question you ask is a form of entrapment.

MANZINI: A form of entrapment?

HELENA: A trick?

MANZINI: Fair enough. My life is a bag of tricks.

HELENA: You say that love-making is a form of mind-reading, but it can't be true, for…I have heard it said…that when people make love they sometimes hold one person in their arms and fantasize about somebody else.

MANZINI: Do you?

HELENA: I am afraid that is for me to know and for you to find out.

MANZINI: I hope to find out soon.

HELENA: I don't think so.

MANZIINI: Definitely. In a while you will leave this room, you will drive home…in a white Volkswagen that is three years old, when you open your door, your little white cat named Zia will come forward to greet you…

HELENA: How do you know about Zia?

MANZINI: I am afraid that is for me to know and for your to find out.

HELENA: You have had me investigated.

MANZINI: Investigated? Why would I have you investigated? Did I know that you would come backstage to interrogate me?

HELENA: The word is *interview*, not *interrogate*.

MANZINI: I suppose that depends upon which side of the fence you are on.

HELENA: Of course you knew I was coming backstage to see you. The paper called and arranged it. It was all arranged.

MANZINI: Believe me, Ms. Michaelides, I am not wealthy enough to pay people to investigate everyone who comes to interview me...Just so I could impress them...

HELENA: You have friends in high places...

MANZINI: My wife has friends, yes...But friends are friends...

HELENA: You world travelers are all alike. You think we Greeks are very gullible.

MANZINI: Everybody in the world is gullible, my dear...

HELENA: I am not *your dear*...

MANZINI: We all want the impossible to happen so much that we are prepared to believe anything. We go a thousand psychic miles out of our way to make the impossible happen.

HELENA: You had some friend provide you with information about my personal life...a few details about my car, where I live, my Cat, my friend Tom...and you pass all this off as second sight. You merely play Sherlock Holmes and call it mind-reading.

MANZINI: *(stung)* Just as you like writing things down and calling it reporting.

HELENA: I do not pretend that is something it is not.

MANZINI: That's true. Yes, that's true. But you doubt me every step of the way.

He holds out the bottle of champagne.

HELENA: No more for me, thank you.

MANZINI: Can I offer you anything?

HELENA: Will you answer one more question for me before I go?

MANZINI: Of course. We have no secrets from one another.

HELENA: It seems that I have no secrets from you.

Manzini fills her champagne glass.

HELENA: You are trying to take advantage of me.

MANZINI: Naturally. We take advantage of each other.

68

HELENA: I would like to ask you about your eye.

MANZINI: My good one, or my bad one?

HELENA: The one covered by the white patch.

MANZINI: Ah, my good one.

HELENA: Do you mind if I ask how you lost it?

MANZINI: I said I wouldn't mind. But why should I waste my breath if you won't believe me?

HELENA: Just because I do not believe one thing, it does not mean I doubt all things.

MANZINI: Yes, but you doubt the very fabric of my life…Believe me when I tell you that when you reach home, you will become more and more intrigued about our little conversation, and you will decide to invite my wife and I to supper tomorrow night, and of course we shall accept, but of course my wife will come down with a splitting head-ache. One of those terrible migraines that so frequently attack her, but I will arrive on your doorstep, delivering you a bouquet of daisies, and your cat Zia will greet me, and since animals trust me, you will take that for a good sign, and one thing will lead to another.

HELENA: And now you claim to read the future…

MANZINI: Not *the* future….My future…Or at least my short future with you…

HELENA: And what about Tom…

MANZINI: I guess that will depend whether he is the jealous type or not, won't it? Is he the jealous type?

HELENA: I suppose that will depend whether I tell him or not, won't it?

MANZINI: Some people know things without being told. That is my specialty.

HELENA: And my specialty is being told. *(She reaches for her coat)*.

MANZINI: I have told you all I know. There are no secrets between us.

HELENA: That would be a living hell, for two people to have no secrets from one another.

MANZINI: It is....

HELENA: *(puts on her coat)* And the eye?

MANZINI: We were in Berlin, doing our act, and one afternoon I decided to take in a film. Thea was down with one of her excruciating head-aches, and I had to get away. It was the day of showing OLIVER TWIST, and since I have always been a fan of Dickens, I decided to go. Unfortunately, some of the radical groups decided that the film was anti-Semitic, and decided to use the film as a politically rallying point...I guess it is '47, we're talking about, or '48...So feelings were running pretty high, as you can well imagine...and so there I was sitting in the theater, when people began throwing stones at the screen...I don't think they really cared about the Jews, but it was just some group that wanted to make the Jews look bad, get them into the newspapers as rabble-rousers, that sort of thing...and as I tried to make my exit, a stone got me squarely in the eye...So now I am the one-eyed lover...afraid of going blind...

HELENA: Well, thank you, Mr. Manzini. I really do appreciate our talk...the information...I will make certain that you receive a copy of the story when it appears...

MANZINI: Let me walk you out...

HELENA: That won't be necessary...

MANZINI: No, no...I really want to confirm the license plate numbers on your Volkswagen...Do you want me to tell you what it is...

HELENA: The Nine of Clubs...

MANZINI: Exactly what I was thinking...You wouldn't want to give me a ride to the airport tomorrow morning, would you?

The two exit. The stage is left empty for a moment, and the lights go down.

Scene 2

Several hours later. The Great Manzini is sleeping in the stage left chair. The book of poems is opened in his lap.

Thea Kapsakis, the second half of the Great Manzinis, enters. Because of injuries sustained many years before in an automobile accident, she uses two walking canes, she moves slowly but with great pride and confidence. She is dressed in a flowing gown, with a gleaming tiara upon her mane of red hair. She and her husband are approximately the same age, though it is altogether possible that Thea is a few years older. In any case, she is not a small woman, not in stature, nor in presence.

She walks downstage, stops. She uses one cane to tap her husband upon the leg.

THEA: Wake up! I knew you would be here, waiting for me.

Manzini is roused from his uncomfortable sleep.

THEA: Andrea's driver took me to the hotel, but when I saw that you weren't in your room, I took a cab here. *(She studies the empty champagne bottle).* You drank too much and passed out.

MANZINI: What time is it?

Thea crosses to a window and looks out.

THEA: You can see the clock in the square.

MANZINI: I did not pass out.

THEA: Almost six.

MANZINI: Ah.

THEA: *(turning back to her husband)* Ah!

MANZINI: A.M. or P.M.?

THEA: Where are your shoes? You have over-stayed your welcome…And the patch. You have been sleeping with the patch on your eye.

He removes the patch from his eye. He has two good eyes.

THEA: The doctor tells you it is bad for you. It cuts off circulation. What good is an eye with no blood reaching it?

MANZINI: And yet you criticize me for having blood-shot eyes.

THEA: Not I, my sweet. Not I. When do I ever criticize you?

MANZINI: And you? Did you over-stay your welcome?

THEA: Of course not. They begged me to stay.

MANZINI: They?

THEA: They. All of them.

MANZINI: I love it when you go off with one man and he becomes plural.

THEA: It describes my marriage to you in a nutshell, my dear…We went to Andrea's house. It was his first night back there in weeks.

MANZINI; That is a good sign.

THEA: It is, isn't it? That he is confident enough to go back home.

MANZINI: With all the unrest in the army.

THEA: It's the elections. He is very hopeful. We are set for Thessaloniki on the 28th. We are engaged to entertain some very wealthy people.

MANZINI: There are no wealthy people in Thessaloniki.

THEA: Andreas is quite excited about it.

MANZINI: Yes, it is always a good idea to mix magic and politics. Especially in Greece. That is what makes Greek politics so unique…*(Locates an opened bottle of champagne)* There is some champagne left.

THEA: I am not partial to warm champagne.

MANZINI: *(tasting it)* It hasn't gone flat.

THEA: I have a terrible feeling we are going to lose our freedom.

MANZINI: We have been through all that. It just means that we're growing old, that's all. When you're young, you think freedom is one thing; when you've been through enough sorrow, you see freedom as something else. Whatever it is, freedom is never what the people in power tell you it is.

THEA: Oh, you're so far above us all.

MANZINI: No, I am not. I just want to change my clothes, so you might as well sit down.

THEA: I don't think we should go back to the hotel. I don't have the same confidence in the future that Andreas has. But what could I tell them?

MANZINI: I am still going to change my clothes.

THEA: We should go straight to Thessaloniki.

MANZINI: I hate falling asleep in my eye-patch. It leaves those elastic marks upon my skin. Can you see them?

THEA: *(studying his face)* Consider them wrinkles.

MANZINI: Of course. Why not. What good is talking politics all night if all people do is get wrinkles. Where is the legislation to ban growing old?

THEA: There was a king who made it against the law to grow old.

MANZINI: What happened to such a wise king?

THEA: He ordered all his subjects put to death. Fortunately, the law was not easily enforced because the generals could never prove that anyone was really growing older. White hair was no proof. Wrinkles were no proof. Trembling hands were no proof, especially whenever a general breathed, hands trembled.

MANZINI: I am sorry I asked.

THEA: Yes, dear Henry, I am sorry too.

MANZINI: Politics here, politics there, and not a drop to drink.

THEA: The only real proof that the people were growing old was that they were willing to tolerate such an unfair law.

MANZINI: It does sound as if you had a most fascinating evening.

THEA: Believe me, my love, Andreas and his friends were far more interested in me than they were in politics. At least for a few moments. Most of the conversation settled on devils and demons.

MANZINI: It is good that you steered the topics around to some area you felt comfortable with.

THEA: Yes, wasn't it.

MANZINI: And what did you tell them about me.

THEA: Nothing about you.

MANZINI: Then I would have been bored.

THEA: What could I say? I said there are demons all about us. They possess our thought, but they do not gain entry to our souls. Our spirit is air. *Spiritus.*

MANZINI: And in my case, some hot spiritus.

THEA: And then someone asked Andreas whether Papadopoulos could be such a demon, but no one laughed.

MANZINI: I think he needed guests because he did not want to be alone.

THEA: And then some idiot woman dared to ask me to read her palm, as if I indulged in such hocus-pocus.

MANZINI: I should have been there to protect you.

THEA: Yes, you should have.

MANZINI: But if I had gone along, we would have been called upon to perform, and how could we have said no.

THEA: And saying *no* is not the strongest element in our characters.

MANZINI: We are not of the nay-saying variety.

THEA: While we are on the subject, did you seduce that young reporter....Helena...What was her name?

MANZINI: Michaelides. How willing you are to block out names.

THEA: How willing you are to let them in. Well, did you?

MANZINI: I did not. Otherwise you would not have found me here, would you?

THEA: What went wrong? You had enough facts to impress her with your occult powers.

MANZINI: Nothing went wrong. Why must everything have to happen overnight?

THEA: Because everything in life does happen overnight. Your seductions must be losing some of their qualities around the edges. What story did you tell her about losing your eye. Did you lose it in a duel, this time? Or, fighting for the resistance

MANZINI: Oliver Twist.

THEA: That's the problem. You should have chosen a more heroic tale.

MANZINI: Modern women are not impressed by heroism, Thea.

THEA: They should be. Everyone should be impressed by heroism.

MANZINI: It has so completely vanished from the modern world, that no one would recognize true heroism anymore...It's just another brand of public-relations.

THEA: Spare us. I know what you're thinking before you say it.

MANZINI: You went by the hotel, yes?

THEA: I said I did.

MANZINI: Did you check for messages?

THEA: I always do. You were expecting a billet-doux from your latest conquest?

MANZINI: There was no conquest. There was hardly a climb up the mountain.

THEA: How sad.

MANZINI: Sad? What's sad about it?

THEA: It distorts the focus of your life.

MANZINI: And what should I focus upon? You?

THEA: You could do worse.

MANZINI: I have done worse.

THEA: Besides it is me, no matter how many times you deny it.

MANZINI: I deny it.

THEA: Your black socks are on top of the dresser.

MANZINI: Of course they are. I know where they are.

THEA: You were standing there wondering what you had done with them.

MANZINI: I was standing there wondering where I mislaid my whole goddamn life. Can you locate that, using all your marvelous powers?

THEA: *(Quoting Themelis)* "Outside of us things die."

MANZINI: Screw Themelis. Inside of us, things dies also. That's where all the cunning deaths appear. Inside us. Inside.

THEA: "No matter where you walk at night you hear
Something like a whisper coming out
Of streets you have never walked upon."

MANZINI: It's a new world now. Poetry does not stitch up the wounds anymore.

THEA: Have I wounded you again. You don't go to parties with me...

MANZINI: Because all your friends discuss is politics.

THEA: You don't go because you want your own air to breathe. That's what you were really thinking.

MANZINI: Yes, that's what I was really thinking. As you so well know, you who know my own thoughts better than I do.

THEA: So breathe, my love, breathe. Thrust your head out the window and draw in great gulps, draughts of free air.

MANZINI: I breathe by thinking. That's what you have taken from me.

THEA: And when I came in here a moment ago, you were dreaming.

MANZINI: Yes, I was dreaming. I breathe by dreaming. In that I am like your countrymen.

THEA: You were in a small room with Helena.

MANZINI: Helena?

THEA: Your journalist.

MANZINI: I had forgotten her name.

THEA: I give her name back to you. Take it. It is free of charge.

MANZINI: And what was I doing in this small room, of which I have no memory. My memory is going.

THEA: You slipped on three code words.

MANZINI: We shall rehearse. Tomorrow. First thing.

THEA: You had made love to Helena, and you were starting out the door just as I was coming in, and we collided, and you knocked me backwards. I lost my balance and I went tumbling down a long flight of stairs. And I was lying there, my neck broken. And you stood at the top of the stairs, weeping.

MANZINI: Weeping?

THEA: Yes, you were sobbing your entire soul out, devastated that you had lost me, that you had pushed me out of your life.

MANZINI: That is what it must mean, obviously.

THEA: Obviously.

MANZINI: Not even my dreams are my own.

THEA: You forget them. I give you back to you.

MANZINI: One doesn't enjoy to have one's dream passed through another mind.

THEA: Just as I give you this.

Thea hands her husband an envelope.

MANZINI: What is this?

THEA: You asked if I checked for messages at the hotel.

MANZINI: You said there were none.

THEA: None from Helena. Just this letter from our daughter.

MANZINI: Popi?

THEA: Unless we have a daughter I know nothing about.

MANZINI: I would like one thing in life you know nothing about.

THEA: She is fine.

MANZINI: How is she?

THEA: You remember that woman who lived with her in the hotel?

MANZINI: Any news about the Count?

THEA: That woman who was living with that imposter called the Count, who was no more a Count than the Pope is Jewish…

MANZINI: That too is merely a matter of time.

THEA: The Count walked out on her. Popi says that the woman climbed into her bath-tub, drowned her puppy…

MANZINI: Not the little puppy….

THEA: Drowned the two parrots…

MANZINI: Even the parrots?

THEA: And then she slashed her wrists.

MANZINI: The one that spoke all the naughty words…

THEA: The parrot, you mean. The one parrot that spoke the naughty words, thus shocking the other parrot into a kind of vocal paralysis.

MANZINI: That parrot knew no bounds of decency.

THEA: The Count betrayed her.

MANZINI: But why would she kill herself?

THEA: Took her jewelry, everything. Walked out the door. But, Harry, if you are going to slash your wrists, why drag down the poor innocent dogs and parrots? It's messy, don't you think?

MANZINI: Do I think?

THEA: Of course you, Harry. You try anyway.

MANZINI: And what does our daughter want from us this time?

THEA: She is arriving in just a little while. I have the driver waiting, and I am on the way to the airport to pick her up. You are merely delaying things.

MANZINI: Go ahead without me.

THEA: I am always going ahead without you. You are always lingering. Holding back.

MANZINI: I want out.

THEA: It's a free world. Popi will accompany me to Thessaloniki. But of course you want to go home.

MANZINI: I want to go home.

THEA: But where is home. Where is home? This used to be home. My family, relatives, friends. But you have upset all that.

MANZINI: It is my fault. I take full blame.

THEA: Of course you do, Harry. Of course you do. I married a martyr.

MANZINI: I don't want to hear anymore.

THEA: Show us your stigmata, Harry.

MANZINI: Would you be quiet for a change? I would like quiet. I would like silence. You with your stories of parrots and counts and politics and spirits. I like sleeping in these chairs, taking refuge into dreams.

THEA: Where over and over you push me out the door and down the steps and onto the landing where I lay with my neck broken. Paralyzed forever, except of course that God compensates the broken. I can wander in and out of your thoughts at will.

MANZINI: The worse kind of thievery of all.

THEA: Not thievery, Harry. Love.

MANZINI: How can you call it love?

THEA: It is what the human race has longed for. Each one of us wants another person we can be on perfect terms with, whose thoughts we know, whose thoughts we share. But no. Not you. Not you.

MANZINI: We long for someone to share our most intimate thoughts with. How true.

THEA: It's not two bodies locked - together in the dark. It's two minds locked together in absolute confidence. Trust. No secrets from one another.

MANZINI: I have nothing to share with you, because it is all yours to trespass upon. I have no secrets from you. No, none. And the entire world thinks we are a fake.

THEA: We do have our code, Harry.

MANZINI: In case your mind should go blank. But it never has. It never will. You are afraid of your mind losing its powers, whereas I...I long for my mind to go blank. Completely blank. Then there will be no thoughts for you to read. God, I pray for it!

THEA: I shall be like an explorer lost in a great white snowstorm.

MANZINI: You shall be like an explorer in a great white snowstorm.

THEA: We have our codes and our fiction, like any other marriage.

MANZINI: Yes, yes. Our fiction.

THEA: How we climbed out of a car crash into show-business history. What a laugh.

MANZINI: No one is laughing, Thea.

THEA: But it was me lying on the landing paralyzed. But I forgive you, Harry. I really do.

MANZINI: Do you?

THEA: Of course I do. Do you think I enjoy wandering about your thoughts. I try to blot them out, but they come to me. Just as when we are lying together in the dark, it is your dreams that I dream. I want my own. Don't you think I would want my own?

MANZINI: No comment.

THEA: Not necessary. Now you are thinking how you would like to walk away from me, walk through that door and never come back. But you always do come back. You go away and come back. What does it matter to me where you are? We have a true marriage. I read your thoughts from afar.

MANZINI: I turn the corner and Big Brother is watching me.

THEA: Not Big Brother, Harry. Never Big Brother. Not even Sister.

MANZINI: It's like escaping from prison.

THEA: Is it?

MANZINI: One day I shall make it over the wall.

THEA: One more conquest, and you think I shall be able to blot Thea from my mind, but when am I ever far from your thoughts?

MANZINI: Now. Now. This very instant. I am not thinking of you at all.

THEA: Of course not, Harry. Of course not. How paradoxical of you not to think of me and yet to refer to me. You are like the Alchemist....

THEA AND MANZINI: *(Together)* Who must not think of the word *Rhinoceros* when trying to make gold.

THEA: It is a wonderful feeling, Harry, to know that there is one other human being in the world whose mind I know, whose mind I know as well as my own.

MANZINI: I suppose it is. But from this side...

THEA: Yes, my beloved Harry, we know. It is....

MANZINI: Hell.

THEA: Well, Harry, I must not keep Popi waiting. The Athens airport is a worse hell than anything you can possibly imagine. You will join us in Thessaloniki on the 28th.

MANZINI: We'll see.

THEA: Yes, we shall see.

With great difficulty, Thea exits. Manzini crosses to one of the chairs, picks up a newspaper and settles down to read.

MANZINI: Yes, yes, yes. Tomorrow, we must practice the code my dear.

Helena Michaelides appears at the door.

HELENA: Harry?

MANZINI: *(glancing at his watch)* Right on time.

HELENA: Yes, Harry. I have come to fetch you.

Manzini stands up, holds out his hands toward her.

Lights out.

End of play.

PERILOUS SEAS

At center stage is a sailboat with sails flapping in the wind. Or if this cannot be brought into reality, the set designer may create the abstraction of such a boat, using the floor of the stage and billowing sheets. Sometimes on the sail we shall see flitting images of stars and galaxies. We hear the sound of the ocean. There should be a sense enchantment.

SCENE ONE: DAY

Claire stands all alone on the sailing boat under a panoply of clouds. There is music in what we cannot see. Banister enters with two mugs of coffee. He hands Claire one.

BANNISTER: Contemplating the sky, are we?

CLAIRE: Wondering exactly what is over our heads.....Behind all this blue, there are stars. I know it.

BANNISTER: *(flirting)* Why you're going to marry Jack and not me is something I shall never understand.... It can't be because he owns this yacht, and I don't.

Jack Lieberman, the owner and skipper of this yacht, enters. He is in his early forties, dressed in fashionable jacket and sailing whites.

LIEBERMAN" *(such exuberance)* This is the life, isn't it? Free and unfettered, going this way and that, like a twelve-tone symphony, whichever way the winds blow.

BANNISTER: *(such exuberance)* Aye, Aye, Sir. Nothing better in life than freedom to sail this way and that, guided only by the winds of our imagination.

CLAIRE: *(such exuberance, overlapping)* Foretackle the main sail, pulverize the jib, pearl one, haul in the yardarm, and curry the anchorite.

LIEBERMAN: *(at various sailing tasks too arcane to explain)* Why just before dawn, while you both were sleeping, I tossed out my line and pulled in a refrigerator.

CLAIRE: *(such exuberance, overlapping)* Fringe the topsail, Hem the bowstitch, shiver may earlobes.

BANNISTER: *(at various sailing tasks too arcane to explain)* How many pounds?

LIEBERMAN: *(at various sailing tasks too arcane to explain)* It must have weighed 300 pounds.

CLAIRE: *(at various sailing tasks too arcane to explain)* Is that a record catch for a refrigerator?

LIEBERMAN: A self-defrosting one. Yes. On an 8 pound test line, yes. But you won't guess what was inside the refrigerator.

BANNISTER: The complete words of Kipling.

LIEBERMAN: A curious guess.

BANNISTER: It's what I always guess. Someday, mark my words, I shall be right.

CLAIRE: *(running up sailing pennants)* What was inside the refrigerator?

LIEBERMAN: A dead body.

CLAIRE: *(stopped in her tracks)* I don't believe you.

BANNISTER: A dead body? Jack's putting us on.

LIEBERMAN: No, I am not. I'm telling you it was a dead body. A black man wrapped in head to foot in tin-foil. He had been shot through the forehead.

CLAIRE: What did you do?

LIEBERMAN: Threw him back, of course. I had already caught my quota of dead bodies in refrigerators. I thought I would leave him for some other sports person to recover from the perilous seas.

BANNISTER: Quite right. Absolutely the right thing to do.

CLAIRE: Why is that the correct thing to do?

BANNISTER: Isn't it obvious? If you bring home a dead body in a refrigerator, it's all anybody will talk about. For days on end. You may wish to talk about the paintings of Dufy, the power of the imagination to uproot reality and set our lives on several different courses at once, or you may wish to recite passages from Keats, "She stood in tears amid the alien corn/ The same thast ofttimes hath/ Charmed magic casements, opening on the foam/ Of perilous seas in faery forlorn" all anybody will say is: "Forget the perilous seas and tell us about the dead body in the refrigerator.

LIEBERMAN: And what is there to say about it?

CLAIRE: It wasn't my first husband by any chance? The body in the refrigerator, I mean.

LIEBERMAN: *(bringing forth a martini pitcher in a tray with glasses)* What would make you think so?...Martinis?

CLAIRE: Yes, thank you. Because of the description. It sounded so much like the kind of things he would do. Wrap himself in tinfoil and get himself shot through the forehead....

BANNISTER: *(taking a martini)* Also no matter where Claire and I would go, even if it were out sailing on the most splendid of late fall days, Roger would always turn up in the most unexpected places just to ruin our moods.

CLAIRE: In college, Roger was voted the one most likely to end up dead in a refrigerator. It was, in fact, a category which he won unanimously.

BANNISTER: It sounds as if your college were more into tinfoil than into Kierkegaard.

CLAIRE: Do we have much longer to sail?

LIEBERMAN: It depends.

CLAIRE: Depends on what?

LIEBERMAN: On moods. The mood of the winds, the mood of the perilous seas, the mood of the person at the tiller, the moods of the tides. The moods of the planets shifting over our heads, the moods of the crew, the moods of the passengers.

BANNISTER: The sky is beginning to grow dark.

CLAIRE: I thought that sailing was more of a science. I didn't realize it was so emotional.

LIEBERMAN: Suppose there were a beautiful island, inhabited only with enchantment, would you steer toward her?

CLAIRE: Of course.

LIEBERMAN: But suppose there was another island equally enchanted and not quite as near. Now which one would you sail for?

BANNISTER: The farthest one.

CLAIRE: The nearest one. Then when you tired of its enchantment, you could always sail on to the next one.

BANNISTER: *(pointing)* Now there is a sport....

CLAIRE: Where?

BANNISTER: Off the stern or the starboard port.... *(points)* See them? A man and woman, stark naked on the back of a whale, making love.

CLAIRE: Astonishing. I have never seen anything like it.... I mean I've never seen that species of whale before.

LIEBERMAN: Thar she blows!

BANNISTER: The whale doesn't seem to mind.

CLAIRE: If I were a whale, I am not certain how I would feel about humans using me as a kind of blubbery waterbed.

BANNISTER: I thought love-making was a science. I didn't realize it was so emotional.

LIEBERMAN: It seems very probable, you know. That a naked man and a naked woman would just end up on the back of a whale in the middle of perilous seas.

BANNISTER: I would give you odds of twenty to one against that sort of thing happening more than once in the life of any couple.

A single snowflake falls from the sky.

LIEBERMAN: A blizzard!

BANNISTER: Only one miserable snowflake. No need to exaggerate.

LIEBERMAN: I suppose you're the kind who says "only one miserable whale with a lovemaking couple on its back." What do you want? An entire pod? Exaggeration is what it's all about my dear man. We exaggerate our moods, our accomplishments, our failures. There is the life we have led, and the life we have thought we have led. And the life we would have led, that is if everything went out way. We even exaggerate the fear of our own death, as it if mattered.

CLAIRE: Look, he's thrown her off... I mean the whale has thrown her off. She's toppled into the sea.

BANNISTER: Toss her a life-preserver.

CLAIRE: She's swimming this way.

BANNISTER: How do you know it's a he?

CLAIRE: It's a she. Can't you tell? She's naked.

BANNISTER: I'm talking about the whale.

CLAIRE: I don't know anything about the sec of whales. What kind of a life do you think I've led?

BANNISTER: Didn't Catherine the Great make love to a whale once? Had it lowered by means of pully and tackle on to her bed.

CLAIRE: Stop it. You're being disgusting.

Sound of thunder and lightning.

LIEBERMAN: I can't find the life preserver... *(Tosses his martini pitcher overboard)* Here, hold on to this.

BANNISTER: I don't think a martini pitcher will be much help.

LIEBERMAN: In times of stress, a dry martini has always been a great help to me.

We see an arm coming over the side of the boat. And then the top of a head. Then a women fully dressed in a wet formal gown. This is Leila Caron, a dark-haired French beauty.

LEILA: Help!

The others help her on board.

BANNISTER: Don't worry. You're safe now.

LEILA: Safe? I was perfectly safe until someone hit me in the head with a martini pitcher.

LIEBERMAN: But you're fully dressed.

LEILA: *(squeezing water from her hair)* Of course, I'm fully dressed. What do you want me to do? Appear nude before perfect strangers? I don't even appear nude before my parents. Thank God, I managed to pull on some clothes while swimming to your boat.

BANNISTER: You're a skillful swimmer.

LEILA: No. I'm a skillful dresser.

LIEBERMAN: I'd offer you a martini but I see you didn't bring the pitcher back with you.

LEILA: Sorry. I did the best I could....My name is Leila. Leila Caron.

LIEBERMAN: I'm Jack Lieberman, and these are my friends Edgar Bannister and Claire Maleski.

Lightning flashes.

LIEBERMAN: *(at the wheel)* There's going to be a storm. We should get to shore. If there is any shore. I have always wondered. Is there any shore? I've never seen any shore in my lifetime.

BANNISTER: What about your friend on the whale? Should we rescue him?

LEILA: No. Don't worry about Frederich. It's his whale.

BANNISTER: He owns a whale?

LEILA: He owns most of the ocean as far as I can tell.

LIEBERMAN: No one owns the ocean.

LEILA: Just the bottom rights then.

BANNISTER: Talking about bottom rights, what were you two doing on the back of the whale? ..I mean, we know what you were doing, but how did you two get there? You must admit it was an extraordinary sight.

LEILA: You were watching us?

CLAIRE: It was a choice between watching you and your friend, and looking at a vast expanse of dark sky.

BANNISTER: I believe it was the only entertainment for miles around.

LIEBERMAN: And he's talking nautical miles.

LEILA: I'm so embarrassed.

CLAIRE: It's nothing to be embarrassed about. People do it all the time...Just not on the back of whales....Not that I know if. Of course, I have never been this far away from shore before.

LIEBERMAN: We didn't use binoculars, if that's any comfort.

LEILA: What's so wrong with looking at a vast expanse of shy? A vast expanse of shy can be completely satisfying. Why must people's minds always be on things beneath them.

LIEBERMAN: As soon as I locate a new pitcher, I'm mixing us all batch of martinis.

CLAIRE: We didn't look that long.

LEILA: It didn't last that long.

LIEBERMAN: It does not bode well to be sober in such a serious world. Or as some Puritan preacher once told his congregation, "It spoils the bow to keep it always bent, and the viol of always strained up."

LEILA: Just whose viol was he talking about?

BANNISTER: We hate to be curious, Ms. Caron.

LEILA: No you don't. You love to be curious…. Curiosity certainly got me into this strange dilemma, all right…. Don't you just hate it when you get a strange notion in your head and it gets you in all sorts of trouble?

BANNISTER: What else in there?

LEILA: All right, if you insist, I'll tell you how Frederich and I ended up on the back of the whale.

LIEBERMAN: Thank you. I'll be indebted to you for the rest of my life… Otherwise I would be forced to make up things that have nothing to do with reality… Please, take this martini. It's shaken not stirred.

LEILA: Just like my love life…. Shaken, but not stirred…. You know how life is. Sometimes you get bored with it all. I was desperate for some excitement, some new adventure, thrills, chills, and spills, and Frederich owns Whale World. So to win my affections, he gave me the whale as a gift, and we would ride on its back in the huge tank at Whale World. The Whale and I took an instant liking to one another. I don't think it likes to be separated from me. Then for some reason, two days ago the whale made a thunderous leap, over the seawall, into the perilous seas, with Frederich and I holding onto the harness for dear life. Of course, we let go as soon as we dared, swam toward Frederich's Yacht, and we took off in mad pursuit of the whale. Unfortunately, my husband saw me sailing off in Frederich's yacht, and so in his speedboat, he followed us to a spot not far from here. Frederich, in a jealous rage, shot my husband through the forehead wrapped him in tinfoil and stuffed him into a refrigerator and dumped him to the bottom of the perilous sea. Naturally watching so much violence in dangerous situations gets the erotic juices flowing and so in a fit of temporary madness, after having caught up with our whale, we climbed aboard the creature's back and started to make love. At first it was a bit slippery, but there is a rocking and rolling motion that adds to the ecstasy, and of course the whale had that huge harness around him, which gave us something to hold onto in the swells… The only problem is concentration, because we have to keep our eyes out for Japanese whaling ships. Frederich's viol was nearly harpooned….at a most critical moment.

CLAIRE: *(gulps the martini)* God!

BANNISTER: *(gulps the martini)* God!

LIEBERMAN: *(gulps the martini)* It's going to be night soon…. Come below…We could use some merriment to prepare us for the storms to come.

BANNISTER: The Reverend Benjamin Coleman of Boston once preached a sermon in Puritan Massachusetts which he contended that "We daily need some respite & diversion, without which we dull our powers; a little intermission sharpens 'em again."

A little intermission until night settles over the perilous seas.

SCENE TWO: NIGHT

Claire stands all alone on the sailing boat under panoply of stars. Night music in what we cannot see. Banister enters with two filled champagne glasses. He hands Claire one.

BANNISTER: Contemplating the stars, are we?

CLAIRE: Wondering exactly what is over our heads.

BANNISTER: Well, the dreams of the day are not the dreams of the night, are they? See! *(points toward the night sky)* There's the whale, the constellation Cetus, with its bright star Mira Ceti, the first variable star to be so recognized.

CLAIRE: How comforting to know there is a whale over our heads, and a whale under our feet.

BANNISTER: An ocean of unknown over our heads; an ocean of unknown below our feet…Strange though.

CLAIRE: What?

BANNISTER: That the sea can sometimes present us with some strange creature, something spiney and lopsided that can make us laugh, but the sky never can. Nothing in the constellations to evoke even a smile, except perhaps the smile of recognition.

CLAIRE: Failing stars, perhaps?

BANNISTER: Not even falling stars. Earth can make us laugh, and oceans, but never what is over our heads, panoply of galaxies whirling, whirling.

CLAIRE: I always thought of astronomy as an exact science. I never realized it was so filled with emotion.

BANNISTEER: It's almost all emotion, or why would be so drawn to it. It is the mystery of the thing. Traveling into ourselves by traveling out far beyond ourselves....A closed universe as it is.

CLAIRE: I don't know. Everything that happened today was so strange, so out of the ordinary.

BANNISTER: *(kisses the back of her neck)* That's what we live for, isn't it?....By the way, where are Jack and Leila?

CLAIRE: I think they went to the stern so Jack can give her mouth to mouth resuscitation.

BANNISTER: *(glancing at his watch)* At this late hour? We pulled her out of the ocean hours ago.

CLAIRE: Better to be safe than sorry, he said.

BANNISTER: I hope he doesn't get too involved.

CLAIRE: Why not? She is very attractive, you know, or she will be once the smell of whale is washed away.

BANNISTER: Well, it will all come to no good. She is a murderer you know. Or the accomplice to one.

CLAIRE: There are the laws of the sea and the laws of the land. The laws of the day and the laws of the night.

BANNISTER: But murder is murder no matter where it happens.

Lightning Flashes.

CLAIRE: There is something about the night that brings out the worst in us.

BANNISTER: Leila's husband was shot in the daytime.

CLAIRE: Then there is something in the day that brings out the worst in us.

BANNISTER: I think it's the basic elements. We have something in the earth on us, something of the sea, something of the sky, and each separate kingdom inspires a different kind of dreaming. The other night I was dreaming I was traveling through the underground of a great city, going from metro to metro to metro. And I was carrying something and I needed to find a locker to store it in. I couldn't stop changing trains and walking down corridor after corridor until I found a storage place. But when I woke up, I could not remember what it was that was so precious that I needed a storage place for it.

CLAIRE: What do you think it was?

BANNISTER: Imagination probably.

The heartbreaking song of a love-sick whale.

CLAIRE: What is that?

BANNISTER: I don't know. I have never quite heard anything like it. It sounds like a love sick whale.

Leila wrapped in a white beach towel enters.

LEILA: Do you hear that?

BANNISTER: How could we miss it?

LEILA: That's Gynt, the whale. He's calling for me. He's heart broken….missing me.

CLAIRE: How can you be certain that it's not Frederich?

LEILA: Oh when a woman reaches a certain age, she can always tell the difference between a man and a whale – even though they are both mammals at heart. (*Calls out to the perilous seas*) Don't fret, honey. I'm coming.

BANNISTER: You are going to swim through all those high waves in the lightning?

LEILA: What choice do I have? After all I did make love on his back?

CLAIRE: I don't think that's much of a commitment, even on the high seas.

LEILA: Jack went below to fetch champagne....Please, tell him, I'll wait for him on the back of the whale. That is if he wants to join me.

CLAIRE: Well, what about Frederich? What are you going to do about him?

LEILA: Oh, my husband was the jealous type, not Frederich....

Sound of love-sick whale.

BANNISTER: The whale misses you that much?

LEILA: Don't worry, my darling, I'm coming.

Leila drops her towel and leaps into the ocean. She is swallowed up in the darkness as she swims toward the whale we can only hear.

BANNISTER: What a woman!

CLAIRE: *(impetuously)* Albert, make love to me.

BANNISTER: Here?

CLAIRE: Yes, right here. On the deck under the stars, surrounded by lightning. And the cry of a love sick whale. I could not think that a night upon the seas under the dangerous stars could be so erotic.

BANNISTER: *(taking her in his arms)* Well, if you insist.

Claire takes banister by the tie and pulls him down with her to the deck of the ship. They start to make love. As they start to undress each other, Lieberman enters, carrying a bucket of iced champagne and two glasses. He steps over the two lovers and goes on.

BANNISTER: Jack, it's not what you think.

LIEBERMAN: No, no, it never is....I say, why don't you two try the back of a whale.

Lieberman goes out in search of Leila.

CLAIRE: That's a lovely idea!

BANNISTER: A good idea is tremendously erotic. Actually, for some philosophers, sex, so much better in theory than in practice. In discussing a theory, one can take so many different position.

CLAIRE: *(stands up)* No, no. Jack's right, as usual...We must try it.

LIEBERMAN: *(returns)* Where did Leila go?

CLAIRE: She swam out to the whale. It seems that the whale misses her.

Sounds of the whale. A concerto?

CLAIRE: Do you hear her?

LIEBERMAN: That's Leila?

BANNISTER: No. I believe, in point of fact, that's the whale.

LIEBERMAN: *(calls over the railing)* Hold on, Leila, I'm coming.

BANNISTER: Jack, are you crazy? You can't swim out there.... There's lightning.

Another snowflake falls from heaven.

BANNISTER: There's snow....There's lightning, There's star light. A veritable blizzard of dangers, real and imaginary,

LIEBERMAN: *(removing his coat and deck shoes)* I can't leave Leila out there all alone with that killer.

BANNISTER: The whale seems friendly enough.

LIEBERMAN: I was talking about Frederich, not the whale. The homicidal madman who shot Leila's husband through the forehead.

BANNISTER: From what I've seen of Leila, you could think of it as a mercy killing. Put the poor man out of his misery.

LIEBERMAN: Don't wait up for me, my dears. I don't know when I shall be back.

BANNISTER: But Jack, Claire and I don't know anything about sailing.

LIEBERMAN: Do the best you can. If all is lost, sail toward enchantment…Or give yourself up to the current. The sea will always take you somewhere..

He dives over the side. We hear the sound of a splash.

LIEBERMAN'S VOICE: *(from the ocean)* Leila, dear, wait for me.

BANNISTER: How's he doing?

CLAIRE: I don't know. It's too dark. I can't see.

BANNISTER: I hate it when the sea is so dark.

CLAIRE: And so perilous.

Lightning flashes, oh hell, add some thunder too. Gynt the Whale trumpets with newfound happiness.

BANNISTER: And lit only by lightning.

The sound of a man and a woman singing opera.

BANNISTER: What's that?

CLAIRE: It sounds like Jack and Leila singing opera – a duet from *Lohengrin.*

BANNISTER: Well, that must be the first. *Lohengrin* performed on the back of a whale!

CLAIRE: No, it's been done before. At La Scala, in 1965, but never in this context.

BANNISTER: Context? What context?

CLAIRE: Sky, stars, sea, snowstorm, and lightning. What more context can you possibly wish for?

BANNISTER: Something a little less heavy on atmosphere, I should think. Besides every star in the sky has a name, as do the creatures of the sea. The problem with your romantics is that you think Naure is generic – flower, earth, rock. Each nameless.

CLAIRE: Don't worry, Jack. I'm coming.

BANNISTER: What are you talking about?

CLAIRE: It's a signal that Jack and I have. That duet from *Lohengrin* is our song.

BANNISTER: If Lohegrin were meant to be sung from the back of a trained whale, Wagner would have written it that way!

CLAIRE: He's saying that he needs me.

BANNISTER: How could you possibly understand what he's singing without a libretto in from of you? That's the trouble with this world. Nature should supply us with a written text!

CLAIRE: *(revealing her swimsuit)* Don't try to stop me. I'm swimming to Jack.

BANNISTER: I'm not trying to stop you, but I don't think the back of a whale can hold that many love-starved humans.... Perhaps you should wire ahead for reservations.

CLAIRE: You're jealous.

BANNISTER: I'm afraid for you. It's too dark out there.

CLAIRE: I'll be guided by the music.

BANNISTER: That's not music. That's Wagner.

CLAIRE: I'm swimming to my true love before he's swallowed alive by Leila. That's all I know.

Claire leaps into the ocean. We hear a splash.

BANNISTER: Claire, come back. It's too dangerous!...What about me? I can't sail safely through this storm....And don't give me any of that phony enchantment stuff. I want latitude and longitude!....God! I just hate it out here. It's so wet...So cold...So uncertain...A fire. I'll build a fire.... *(starts collecting wood)* Why is it that when one little thing out of the ordinary happens, the days falls apart....It must be freezing on the back of the Orca....And smells so blubbery....Somebody's got to hold the fort....Matches. I need matches....Somebody's got to be practical. I mean opera sounds fine in the middle of the night, but what are you going to do in the morning? Who makes breakfast? Who slaughters the hog....or mixes martinis, as the case may be…Never, never, never toss a pitcher of martinis overboard!

We see two male arms over the top of the boat. Then a male form, dripping, partially lifts himself out of the water. He carries a rifle over his shoulders.

FREDERICH: Excuse me. My name is Frederich Von Gehringer, and I'm looking for a woman named Leila….You haven't seen her, by any chance?

BANNISTER: Oh, you poor man! You just missed her. You just swam by her in the black waters….Here let me help you up….Come on to the boat. And get warm. I am building a fire…a lovely, warm, and lasting…

FREDERICH: *(shivering from his swim, he finds Leila's towel)* Ah, a fire…Yes, a fire… I am freezing. But don't burn anything you might want back.

BANNISTER: That is to say real fire….a real light so we can find our way through this perilous night upon this perilous sea.

A lightning flash.

Then lights out.

WHAT I DID TO THE GREAT GOD OF COMEDY & WHAT THE GREAT GOD OF COMEDY DID TO ME

We are in the tiny East Side apartment of Brewer Hopkins, 29 years old, lanky, mostly arms, up-start comedian of village dives and yuk-yuk places of the completely unknown and unwanted. Actually this haven of domestic bliss can be suggested by a simple table, a few wooden chairs, and a lamp with garish shade. Much more furniture would be superfluous. But then most of our lives are superfluous anyway.

Brewer, on his way to take a shower and clad only in a blue bath towel and floppy sandals. He is preparing a monologue to be presented that evening at some coffee-house for comics. He recites a bit of it to us. He crosses to his wife's pocketbook which is on the table. He opens the pocketbook to look for a cigarette.

BREWER: So there I am, buying a life insurance policy at the Pacific All Risk Insurance Company, and the policy is being hustled by some joker named Walter Neff. Walter Neff. Did you ever hear of him? He looks a lot like Fred MacMurray. But I'll tell you one thing though -- it doesn't seem right to be sold Life Insurance by a man who is planning to murder you. It's like being sold groceries by the people who eat all the dinner. But what can I do? It's still the best insurance deal in town. If I get thrown from a train, my wife gets double indemnity.

Brewer's wife Katherine enters. She is shapely, tall, brunette and dressed in a black dress enhanced by a simple string of pearls.

KATHERINE: What are you doing with my pocketbook?

BREWER: I was looking for a cigarette.

KATHERINE: How many times do I have to tell you? I don't like you going through my pocketbook.

She holds out her hand. Brewer, who has been through this scene many times, gives her the pocketbook. She hands him a pack of cigarettes.

BREWER: You got something in there you don't want me to see?

KATHERINE: What's it got to do with you?

BREWER: How do I know? Maybe you're carrying a concealed weapon.

KATHERINE: Maybe I am.

BREWER: I'm only your husband.

KATHERINE: Don't remind me.

BREWER: I don't know why you're making such a big deal out of it. I wasn't prying into your personal effects.

KATHERINE: Perhaps you'll wish you had.

She pulls out a pistol and shoots her husband in the groin. Brewer, writhing in pain, collapses to the floor.

BREWER: God!...What did you do that for?

KATHERINE: No reason.

She replaces the pistol in her pocketbook.

BREWER: All I wanted was a lousy cigarette.

KATHERINE: No reason at all.

BREWER: That's just great.

KATHERINE: What's great?

BREWER: Mad dog killers sometimes manage to come up with a reason. But you...You stand there cool as a cucumber. You shoot your husband in cold blood and think nothing of it.

KATHERINE: You don't know what I'm thinking.

BREWER: Tell me.

KATHERINE: I'm late for an appointment. I'll have to talk to you later.

BREWER: Later I'll be dead.

KATHERINE: Sounds good to me.

BREWER: At least call me an ambulance.

KATHERINE: All right. You're an ambulance.

Katherine goes out the door. As she goes out, the God of Comedy, wearing a three piece blue suit, the mask of comedy. Smoking a cigar through the smiling mouth, and bearing a bald head, enters.

BREWER: Oh that's funny. Really funny. Call me an ambulance. All right, you're an ambulance. Who writes your material? Joe Miller?

Brewer looks up and sees the God of Comedy seated at the table.

BREWER: You're seated in the No Smoking section.

THE GOD OF COMEDY: Sorry.

He stubs out his cigar into a section of grapefruit.

BREWER: Wait a minute.

THE GOD OF COMEDY: What's your problem?

BREWER: What's my problem? My wife has shot me and has left me for dead. Of course for you that might not be a problem at all. Who in the hell are you anyway? And what are you doing here?

THE GOD OF COMEDY: I am the Great God of Comedy, Comedy, from the Greek meaning to revel.

He removes the mask of comedy and sets it on the table.

BREWER: You couldn't have picked a better time to visit?

THE GOD OF COMEDY: Laughter being what it is, I have a very busy schedule.

BREWER: God, I'm going out of my mind. Is this what the final seconds of my life are going to be like?....Will you please tell me who you are?

THE GOD OF COMEDY: I told you who I am.

BREWER: You're not the God of Comedy. Nobody's the God of Comedy.

THE GOD OF COMEDY: The Great God of Comedy.

BREWER: If you were the Great God of Comedy, you would be making billions of dollars on television. You'd be hanging around your swimming pool, not coming into my apartment to take advantage of me while I'm on my last legs...Not even on my legs.

THE GOD OF COMEDY: You think I wear this mask for laughs? It went out of style centuries ago. Permit me to contradict your mad ramblings. I am the Great God of Comedy. That maligned being who has presided over the genius of Aristophanes, Shakespeare, Moliere, Ibsen, Pirandello, Phillips, and you.

BREWER: Ibsen?

THE GOD OF COMEDY: It depends on how you look at things.

BREWER: Hedda Gabler? You call Hedda Gabler a comedy?

THE GOD OF COMEDY: I'm not strong on theory.

BREWER: May I ask you a question?

THE GOD OF COMEDY: Shoot.

BREWER: Shoot? That's a bit tasteless, isn't it?

THE GOD OF COMEDY: Is that your question?

BREWER: No, it's not.

THE GOD OF COMEDY: If you want taste, go to the Great God of Tragedy. He'll depress you, but he'll give you all the taste you want. Plus he'll throw in, at no extra charge, the three unities.

BREWER: All right, I've had it with you. If you're the Great God of Comedy, why didn't you make me funnier?....That's my question.

THE GOD OF COMEDY: Funnier?

BREWER: I'll settle for funny.

THE GOD OF COMEDY: Funny Schmunny.

BREWER: Funny Schmunny? That's your answer?

THE GOD OF COMEDY: Why didn't I make you funny? That's your question?

BREWER: Damn it. I worship you. I wash the very socks you walk in. But I've been out there night after night, year in, year out, and every Tom, Dick and Harry is drawing more money than I am. You made Charlie Chaplin funny. Buster Keaton, Jack Benny...

THE GOD OF COMEDY: And Ibsen.

BREWER: Ibsen if you want. But not me. All I ever wanted to do was to make people laugh!

THE GOD OF COMEDY: Why?

BREWER: Why? What do you mean why?

THE GOD OF COMEDY: Why bother. Leave people alone. They don't need you to make them laugh. They have their own problems.

BREWER: Of course if you put it that way.

THE GOD OF COMEDY: And I do.

BREWER: And you do....You're right. You're absolutely right. Why should I care if complete strangers laugh or not. What's it to me? Let's all sit around all day and be morose. Miserable. We could concentrate on the news of the world. (picks up the newspaper). Here's a pretty little item:

> A woman clutching her 10 month old son
>
> stretched across elevated subway tracks
>
> in Brooklyn early yesterday and an oncoming
>
> train killed her and critically injured her
>
> child, the police said.

There. Does that cheer you up? Is that what you want the world to be?

THE GOD OF COMEDY: I have no control over that.

BREWER: Of course not. If you can't make a peanut butter sandwich, I can't expect you to save the life of a 10 month old child.

THE GOD OF COMEDY: I'm just a very minor God. On Parnassus, Comedy does not rate very high on the list of priorities. I don't dine at the big table overflowing with ambrosia and nectar, waited upon hand and foot by golden robots on wheels. I don't sleep with the Muses, for, although I desire them, they desire not me. And I am given only inferior, second-rate talents to work with.

BREWER: Thanks.

THE GOD OF COMEDY: You're welcome.

Brewer sinks into a chair.

BREWER: You depress me.

THE GOD OF COMEDY: I depress a lot of people.

BREWER: Is that what the Great God of Comedy should do? Depress people? Does that make sense to you?

THE GOD OF COMEDY: It makes sense to me, but then the mind of a God is far beyond ordinary human logic. Besides, in your own way of viewing the world, if things made sense, there would be no need for laughter.

BREWER: I thought you weren't strong on theory.

THE GOD OF COMEDY: Does that sound like a strong theory to you? Look at this way. Whatever you say about Comedy, you can say about Tragedy. But you say it with a smile on your face. If things made sense, tragedy would be obsolete. So would politics for that matter. Philosophy. Television. Cereal.

BREWER: I have a feeling you could go on forever, and I would rather not hear it.

THE GOD OF COMEDY: Why is it that as soon as I sit down with one of my disciples, he or she wishes me to take a vow of silence.

BREWER: You're not exactly a bundle of laughs.

THE GOD OF COMEDY: How you know? On Parnassus I keep everybody in stitches. But, of course, gods have a very low threshold for pain.

BREWER: I wish I could figure this all out.

THE GOD OF COMEDY: And who said Comedy had to be funny all the time? Of course, it's useful if it's funny some of the time...Useful.

BREWER: Just tell me what you want from me.

THE GOD OF COMEDY: For the last few years I had the feeling you wanted something from me.

BREWER: I did. I wanted to dine at the table of the gods and make them laugh.

THE GOD OF COMEDY: Gods don't laugh.

BREWER: Wait a minute. Just a moment ago you said that you kept everybody on Parnassus in stitches.

THE GOD OF COMEDY: That doesn't mean they laugh. I say things and they think about. Which is something I wish you would do. Gods don't laugh. Animals don't laugh. Only the small pathetic trunk on two legs trembling. I commend you to your copy of *Tractatus Coislinanus*.

BREWER: Please! You're giving me a headache. It's not that I'm ungrateful for your bringing me back to life, but, on the other hand, I did make you a sandwich. Considering the value of human life in the 20th Century that may be more than an even trade.

THE GOD OF COMEDY: I'm going to tell you why I'm here.

BREWER: Thank God!

THE GOD OF COMEDY: You're welcome.

He brings forth some badly mimeographed pages.

THE GOD OF COMEDY: I brought you some new material.

BREWER: You've brought me some new material?

THE GOD OF COMEDY: If you repeat everything I say, we're going to be here all night.

BREWER: You mean the Great God of Comedy is bringing me material straight from His own puffy lips? You've changed your mind about me? You're not going to keep me consigned to the basement of the yuk-yuk palaces forever?

THE GOD OF COMEDY: With material straight from the gods,

I'm going to make you famous.

BREWER: You're going to make me famous?

THE GOD OF COMEDY: That's right.

Brewer gives forth a great sigh of relief.

BREWER: At last! I knew that if I worked long enough, if I struggled enough, if I begged, borrowed, and groveled long enough, that at long last my work would be rewarded, that I could not go unrecognized forever. Famous! At last!

THE GOD OF COMEDY: At last, but not in this century.

BREWER: Wait a minute! What do you mean "Not in this Century?"

THE GOD OF COMEDY: As a God I get to see down the long road. I'm going to give you jokes for the next century.

BREWER: You're going to give me jokes for the next century?

THE GOD OF COMEDY: I am not making myself clear? Look, schmnedrik, I need somebod, not necessarily a genius...

BREWER: Thank you.

THE GOD OF COMEDY: ...to lay the groundwork for the future. Comedy is dying. It's sit-coms, and monologues without soul. My worshippers are dying in the streets. The Temple to the Great God of Comedy is either empty or filled with losers. Tragedy gets all the Academy Awards, I want a better house on Olympus. Don't I deserve a swimming pool and golden robots on wheels? Don't answer that. I do. So, through you, I'm giving the world material to resuscitate the sound of laughter. You break the mold. You carve new mood. And when historians come to write the history of comedy...as they will for generations of illiterates to come, you... whatever your name is...

BREWER: Brewer Hopkins...

THE GOD OF COMEDY: Correct. You will be honored for going where no comedian has gone before. They'll cite you for bravery. You'll make Lenny Bruce look like an arch-conservative, a reactionary. You'll be, in your own small way, immortal. Though not with a kiss. Not without a little sacrifice on your part.

BREWER: You're kidding.

THE GOD OF COMEDY: Perhaps we're not talking the same language.

BREWER: But why me?

THE GOD OF COMEDY: Why not you?....You don't want it?

BREWER: I don't know. It's not good for gods and humans to interact. Every story I read, God picks out somebody for a special mission and it leads to disaster...Some schmuck dining by candlelight in the belly of a whale.

The God of Comedy stands up and makes ready to leave.

BREWER: Where are you going?

THE GOD OF COMEDY: I now realize that my material is much too good for you. There are no end of comedians I can share these jokes with. Everybody and his brother wants to be a comedian.

Brewer blocks the exit of the God.

BREWER: *(panicked)* I'm sorry.

THE GOD OF COMEDY: You should be. After all I have done for you.

BREWER: I've been a humble person all my life. There's no need to humiliate me. Just give me a chance. Is that too much to ask.

THE GOD OF COMEDY: All right. Here goes. These are the best jokes any human being can have.

BREWER: Wow!

The God of Comedy reads from the mimeographed sheets.

THE GOD OF COMEDY: You come out on stage and you ask the audience "What goes up the river?"

BREWER: I give up. What goes up the river?

THE GOD OF COMEDY: Huckleberry Finn in an alternate universe.

BRWER: Huckleberry Finn in an alternate universe?

THE GOD OF COMEDY: Please stop doing that.

BREWER: Stop doing what?

THE GOD OF COMEDY: Repeating everything I say. I am a God. I have a photographic memory. All Gods do. That's why it is possible for us to remember every Tom, Dick and Harry who has neglected to sacrifice to us. It's only because you have deigned to burn a candle at the shrine of Comedy that I have taken the time to come here, bring you back to life, and give you my sacred jokes. Now here's one to knock your socks off. What travels faster than the speed of light? A quark on a busman's holiday.

BREWER: I'm sorry.

THE GOD OF COMEDY: Now what's your problem?

BREWER: A quark on a busman's holiday? That's suppose to be funny?

THE GOD OF COMEDY: It will lay them in the aisles. But not in this century.

BREWER: But why do I have to wait so long? Why can't I be funny now? I want to be appreciated now, in my own time, among my own people.

THE GOD OF COMEDY: It's out of my hands.

BREWER: How can it be out of your hands if you are the Great God of Comedy?

THE GOD OF COMEDY: I have no control over the Fates. I'm merely doing the best I can for you. So X-8765B says, "Who was that Tetrahedron I saw you with last night?" So I tell him, "That was no Tetrahedron. That was my mainframe." Of course you're not laughing, because I'm not doing anything with the material. I'm not punching it up. I'm merely reading it off these mimeographed sheets. But of course with material like this you don't have to work at it very hard.

BREWER: Why are you doing this to me?

THE GOD OF COMEDY: What's black and white and red all over? The Death Penalty in a Fire Free Zone.

BREWER: But I don't even know what a Fire Free Zone is.

THE GOD OF COMEDY: You will when the time comes.

BREWER: Who was that Tetrahedron I saw you with last night? That was no Tetrahedron. That was Miss America in an alternate universe.

THE GOD OF COMEDY: Don't tamper with the material. I have refined those lines over centuries. While men and women were killing each other off in every conceivable way, for every conceivable reason, I sat back and polished those suckers. All with the future in mind. Now listen to this one. I'm telling you it's buffo. A Venetian walks over to a member of Satellite 4 and says, "Why are you malchecking the Black hole." And the member of the satellite crew says, "Because on Tuesday, the Humanoid dropped a free electron."

No response from Brewer.

THE GOD OF COMEDY: Don't you get it? Because on Tuesday the Humanoid dropped a free electron!

BREWER: I get it.

THE GOD OF COMEDY: You do?

BREWER: Of course I don't get it. Nobody will get it. I just said it to hear myself talk. I can't believe you are planning to send me out on some naked stage with a joke like that. I'm going to get my head handed to me on a silver platter. You're setting me up for the kill.

THE GOD OF COMEDY: I don't understand what you're complaining about. You were nearly dead when I came in here.

BREWER: I feel more dead than I felt before.

THE GOD OF COMEDY: Why?

BREWER: Because I want people to enjoy me and my work now. Not at some unnamed point in the future. This is the only life I have.

THE GOD OF COMEDY: An artist has many lives. (He persists). Two quarks and a charm were whooping it up in a cyclotron when...

BREWER: You don't know what you're talking about.

THE GOD OF COMEDY: That's no way to talk to a God! Every time you talk to me you should remove your hat, nod your head. Whatever happened to respect?

BREWER: But there won't be any jokes in the future. No funny movies. No high comedies. No television series. Electrodes will be planted into the brains of every human being. Laughter will be electrically and chemically induced and pharmaceutically induced. People will laugh whenever they want to. The people in charge will push buttons, pull levers, change fuses, and zap! --laughter will issue from their subjects puffy lips. And let me tell you something else, Mr. Omniscient...

THE GOD OF COMEDY: What?

BREWER: I'll never stand up and do the kind of jokes you want me to. You understand? You can take your pregnant electrons, your accelerated mainframes, your alternate universes and go somewhere else. I'd kill myself first if I had to deliver those jokes of yours.

THE GOD OF COMEDY: Go ahead.

BREWER: Go ahead and what?

THE GOD OF COMEDY: Go ahead and kill yourself. I'll just come back down here and bring you back to life again and again. I'll prop you up on the stage and whenever words issue from your puffy lips, they will be my words and my jokes.

BREWER: No way!

THE GOD OF COMEDY: Don't cross a God, baby. You'll lose every time. Now let's go over the monologue item by item.

BREWER: Why me? Why couldn't you pick on a happier man. Like Job?

110

THE GOD OF COMEDY: Listen to me, you Fulton fish market of one-liners, quit whining and accept your fate.

BREWER: If I did that I would be in a tragedy.

THE GOD OF COMEDY: We are in a tragedy. We're only trying to make light of it.

BREWER: Not with jokes like these.

THE GOD OF COMEDY: You're nothing but a mole -- a blind mole tunneling toward the future. You understand?

BREWER: I understand.

THE GOD OF COMEDY: You are merely an instrument in the hands of an angry god.

BREWER: I started out as a human being and I end up as a glockenspiel.

THE GOD OF COMEDY: Bend or be broken.

BREWER: Bend or be broken.

THE GOD OF COMEDY: You are a bridge to the future.

BREWER: I am a bridge to the future.

THE GOD OF COMEDY: It's up to you to shake modern audiences out of their television doldrums. Point their snouts in the direction of a Brave New World. The Old World won't do anymore. You are the chosen one.

BREWER: I am the chosen one.

THE GOD OF COMEDY: Eventually the world will catch up with you, and then you shall be looked upon as...

BREWER: An inelegant footnote in the history of comedy.

THE GOD OF COMEDY: No, as a trailblazer. As a man years ahead of his time. Now may I use your bathrooms.

BREWER: Be my guest.

THE GOD OF COMEDY: I am your guest as you, as long as you are in this world or the next, are mine.

BREWER: I can't believe that a god has to go to the bathroom.

THE GOD OF COMEDY: When in Rome, do as the Romans.

The God of Comedy crosses out to the bathroom that Brewer had originally started for but had never reached.

BREWER: When in Rome, do as the Romans. Oh that's clever. Of course not as clever as What has 18 legs and flies? Two waitresses on Venus.

Katherine, dressed as before, but now wearing a fur coat, enters.

BREWER: I hope that this isn't an illusion. A mirage.

KATHERINE: You hope that what isn't an illusion? A mirage?

BREWER: You...my wife...returning to the scene of the crime. Dressed to kill, so to speak.

KATHERINE: Actually I just came back to get your insurance policy. I left it in the top drawer of my dresser. Is it all right with you if I get it?

BREWER: You can't even ask how I am feeling?

KATHERINE: Sorry. How are you feeling?

BREWER: You left me for dead.

KATHERINE: Well, I am leaving you in any case.

BREWER: You are a really cool customer.

KATHERINE: Am I?

BREWER: Look at you just standing there in a fur coat.

KATHERINE: At least I have gotten dressed today.

BREWER: It's difficult to get dressed when someone shoots you and leaves you for dead.

KATHERINE: I'm afraid I wouldn't know.

She crosses out to the bathroom to get the insurance policy.

BREWER: What good is the insurance policy going to do you? I'm still alive... The Pacific All Risk Insurance Company will not be fooled. Am I dreaming this? No, I don't have the imagination to

112

dream this. Yesterday I thought I was happily married. Yesterday I was working on a comedy routine. My life made a kind of sense. But today the roof caves in. Why doesn't life make sense more than one day at a time? The logic of life should stretch through infinity. There should be continuity. Gods shouldn't be in the bathroom and wives shouldn't be taking potshots at their husbands. I thought by making people laugh I could hang on for dear life.

Katherine, clutching the insurance policy, returns.

BREWER: Find it?

KATHERINE: Found it...Now if I can use the bathroom, I'll be off.

BREWER: What's your hurry? Shouldn't we sit down, like adults, and talk things over?

KATHERINE: Can't. Walter is waiting for me in the car.

BREWER: Walter? Who's Walter?

KATHERINE: The one who sold me the insurance policy. Don't you remember?

Katherine starts toward the bathroom.

BREWER: You can't use the bathroom.

KATHERINE: That's mean spirited of you, isn't it?

BREWER: I'm sorry. I meant to say that the God of Comedy is in there. You can go in when he comes out.

KATHERINE: I'm in no mood for jokes.

She goes into the bathroom.

BREWER: You're in no mood for jokes? What kind of mood do you think I'm in?...(*crosses to the bathroom door*). Are you two having a good time in there, or what? What's going on here? Why is my life beginning to sound like a James Cain novel? As soon as life imitates art, that's comedy. Isn't it?...Isn't it?

Katherine comes out of the bathroom clutching a vial of sleeping pills.

KATHERINE: What are you shouting about?

BREWER: What am I shouting about?....What happened to the God of Comedy? Wasn't he in there with you?

KATHERINE: I just went in to get my sleeping pills. I may have trouble sleeping tonight.

BREWER: What did you do to the God of Comedy?

KATHERINE: *(Lights a cigarette)* There's no one in there. I think you're going crazy.

BREWER: You think I'm going crazy? When did I ever pull out a pistol and try to kill somebody?...I won't have any trouble sleeping tonight. I can tell you that. You know why I won't have any trouble sleeping tonight? Because after years of laboring and getting nowhere and being completely unknown, The God of Comedy has come to me directly and has brought me brand new material, material that will catapult me the forefront of the entertainment world.

KATHERINE: Brewer, I am really happy for you. I really am.

BREWER: Just listen to this joke, brought to me by the God of Comedy himself. "Why did the anti-matter cross the road?" The answer: "It didn't. The anti-matter was the road."

KATHERINE: That's suppose to be funny.

BREWER: A couple of hundred years from now.

KATHERINE: Right.

BREWER: Who was that Tetrahedron I saw you with? Why, sir, that was no Tetrahedron. That was my mainframe.

KATHERINE: Please, Brewer, you're giving me a migraine.

BREWER: Oh no I'm not. You have no sense of humor. If you had a sense of humor, you wouldn't have shot me.

KATHERINE: Brewer, I hate to tell you this, but I never found you very funny.

BREWER: No?...Never?...Not even in bed?

Katherine removes her revolver from her pocketbook.

KATHERINE: I don't want to hurt you, Brewer.

BREWER: You don't want to hurt me? Then why are you pointing a gun at my head?

KATHERINE: I am going to put an end to your misery.

BREWER: Misery? You're going to put an end to my misery? Look, please don't do me any favors.

KATHERINE: I won't.

BREWER: I suppose your friend Walter has a better sense of humor.

KATHERINE: Walter is better at everything.

Brewer is hurt. He flails about helplessly.

BREWER: And so the Charm said to the Neutron, "What's an atomic particle like you doing in a place like this?"

KATHERINE: I had such hopes for us, Brewer. I really did. But if I stay with you, I'll never have anything in life I really want.

BREWER: Like what?

KATHERINE: Laughs.

She shoots her husband in the groin. Brewer, writhing in pain once again collapses to the blood-stained floor. Katherine picks up the insurance policy from the pacific all risk insurance company and starts out.

BREWER: Wait! You didn't hear the one about the travelling Humanoid who sleeps with the milk bottle.

She's gone.

BREWER: You'll never cash that insurance policy. Never! Not as long as I live.

The God of Comedy emerges from the bathroom.

BREWER: I am going to live. Right?

The God of Comedy shrugs, crosses to the table, gathers up his mask and his mimeographed monologue of the future.

BREWER: Hey, where were you hiding when Katherine was in

there? Or am I the only human being privileged to see you?...Boy, you gods have it made. You can be invisible anytime you want. I guess that solves a lot of your sexual hang-ups.

THE GOD OF COMEDY: See you around, Mr. Hopkins.

BREWER: Hold it! You can't walk out on me like this.

THE GOD OF COMEDY: Of course I can. I'm a god. I can do almost anything I want to.

BREWER: But I thought we had an agreement.

THE GOD OF COMEDY: We did, but I'm not going to entrust my valuable material to a man who gets himself shot twice in one afternoon.

BREWER: It's not my fault. I didn't do it.

THE GOD OF COMEDY: To paraphrase one of my favorites, Oscar Wilde, to get yourself shot once is an accident; to get yourself shot twice borders on the masochistic.

BREWER: That's a paraphrase?

THE GOD OF COMEDY: It's a reason for ending our association. I thought you had a lot on the ball.

BREWER: Before you go, can't you reach out your hand and cure me....Like you did last time?

THE GOD OF COMEDY: No. You're like the rest of miserable mankind. You'll take my miracles for granted.

BREWER: I won't. I promise.

THE GOD OF COMEDY: Sorry. I gave you the best jokes of the next century and you mangled them.

BREWER: At least call me a doctor.

THE GOD OF COMEDY: All right. You're a doctor...

BREWER: I knew there was something I hate about comedy.

THE GOD OF COMEDY: Everybody hates what he can't take seriously. Well, I'll see you in the next world, Mr. Hopkins. I trust your journey there is not an unpleasant one, though – the boat is often crowded.

BREWER: Oh no you won't. You won't see me at all. Because I'm not going.

THE GOD OF COMEDY: Why did the man of comedy die? To get to the other side.

The God of Comedy exits.

BREWER: That does it! The God of Tragedy gets everything from me from now on. I henceforth worship at the shrine of high seriousness. Man rapes baby and stuffs her into incinerator. Is that what you want? That's what you get. You hear me? I'm not washing your socks any longer.

The lights dim.

BREWER: I'm not washing anybody's socks any longer. Comedy? What good is it?

Lights out.

The End.

FANS

It is D-Day and we are on Omaha Beach, The sounds of war are all around us, as are strands and bales of barbed wire. Lights up on two mud-splattered soldiers crawling, with heads down, toward some objective far ahead of them. They haven't shaved in days, haven't had much sleep, and have seen many of their comrades-in-arms slaughtered. The first soldier is Squeaker Thomas, a white-bread middle-class Protestant from St. Louis. He is almost 21, and is a bit smaller than his companion. He wears glasses. The second soldier is Joseph G. Truett, a 24 yr old Jewish man from the south Bronx. We hear the whine of machine-gun fire. Bombs fall in the distance.

SQUEAKER: The whole thing stinks.

TRUETT: If a cow came up to me now and nuzzled me in the ass, it would drop dead.

SQUEAKER: How can a Jew from the Bronx be talking about cows? You don't know nothing about cows. No self-respecting cow would be caught dead on this beach.

TRUETT: Somehow I expected better from a French beach.

A grenade goes off. Sand blows over them.

SQUEAKER: I never liked beaches. Sand gets into everything. How many times do I have to clean this rifle?

TRUETT: My fourth grade teacher used to ask: Are there more grains of sand on the beach than there are stars in the sky?

SQUEAKER: Which beach?

TRUETT: How do I know which beach? You might as well ask which sky? Or do we all fight under a different one?

Squeaker removes a slightly yellowed, slightly torn newspaper clipping from his shirt pocket.

SQUEAKER: (*reads with reverence*) Gutteridge, Burns, McQuinn, Stephens, Moore, Christman, Kreevich.

Mancuso, Muncrief...

TRUETT: Not again.

SQUEAKER: Yes, again. Gutteridge, Burns, McQuinn, Stephens, Moore, Christman, Kreevich, Mancuso, Muncrief..Muncrief was the pitcher.

He carefully folds the box score and puts it back into his pocket.

TRUETT: You and you line-up for the St. Louis Browns. I hope that clipping stops a bullet for you someday, because that's about the only thing those fielders can stop.

SQUEAKER: It stinks.

TRUETT: They stink.

SQUEAKER: I haven't gotten boxscores in days. You think if you're out here fighting for your country they could get you the baseball scores. What else was radio invented for? Baseball and radio are like Siamese twins.

TRUETT: I can see the Krauts up that hill.

SQUEAKER: Where?

TRUETT: Keep your head down.

SQUEAKER: If my head were any more down it would be in my boots, and that's where my stinking socks are. Stinking and wet socks. Socks with holes in them. Socks only a mother can love on a beach like this. Stinking beach. Wet beach. Beach with holes in it. A French beach only a mother can love.

Sounds of machine-gun fire. Sand shoots up too.

SQUEAKER: (*lifts up and shouts*) You mothers!

TRUETT: They're in that concrete bunker up on the ridge...

SQUEAKER: Where?

TRUETT: Keep your head down.

SQUEAKER: How can I see where you're pointing?

TRUETT: I'm not pointing. I'm going to describe the situation to you like one of those announcers on the Abbott and Costello show.

They crawl forward a few yards.

SQUEAKER: That's another thing that pisses me off. How did we get so far ahead of everybody else?

TRUETT: You know for someone who Eisenhower has chosen to save civilization, you're one big mass of complaints.

SQUEAKER: Haven blew up a German tank and he was chosen as Yank of the Week, so Chesterfield was suppose to send our unit 3,000 cigarettes. Where in the fuck did all those cigarettes go? Who got 'em? I could use a cigarette right now.

TRUETT: They were probably sent to Brisbane and Brisbane put them somewhere safe.

SQUEAKER: Well, if I get hold of Brisbane I'll shove those cigarettes somewhere safe. Somewhere really safe... Which reminds me – where is Brisbane?

TRUETT: Forget Brisbane.

SQUEAKER: How can I forget Brisbane? He's got 3,000 cigarettes to distribute. I'm not going to forget anybody who has 3,000 cigarettes. Some of those cigarettes are mine.

TRUETT: Brisbane bought the farm.

SQUEAKER: When?

TRUETT: He was cut down the first five minutes we hit the beach.

SQUEAKER: You saw him?

TRUETT: Yeah.

SQUEAKER: Shit.

TRUETT: Shit. (*Pause*)

SQUEAKER: You think he told anybody what he did with the cigarettes?

TRUETT: Forget the cigarettes. Just concentrate on crawling close enough to those machine gunners so we can take them out.

SQUEAKER: I wish I were in St. Louis. It could be a Cardinals/Browns World Series this year.

TRUETT: I wish you were in St. Louis too...But I especially wish all those Krauts were St. Louis and not making my life miserable here.

SQUEAKER: I wish you were Bob Feller.

TRUETT: And I wish you were Betty Grable...naked...so where does all wishing this get us?

SQUEAKER: If Bob Feller were here, he could fire a grenade a 100 miles per hour right through that little opening there and blow that Machine Gun nest to kingdom come.

TRUETT: And if Betty Grable stood up naked the Krauts might become American citizens.

SQUEAKER: And that's another thing I hate. The krauts. They don't nothing about baseball. You capture one of them and there's nothing to talk about. They don't give a shit about the Saint Louis Browns.

TRUETT: You can't judge Nazis on the basis that they know nothing about baseball. There's other more important things.

SQUEAKER: My brother-in-law... he gets to see all the games.

TRUETT: Yeah, but he has to fuck your sister, so give him some kind of a break. As if sitting through St. Louis games is a break. Unless it's the Cardinals. Then he can see Musial.

More gunfire nearby.

TRUETT: St. Louis Browns fans aren't worth pig shit. I'm telling you that if I had to choose between staying in these wet clothes another week and having to watch the Browns play baseball, it would be a toss-up.

SQUEAKER: Keep your head down.

TRUETT: No, When you go to a Browns game, that's when *you* keep your head down. It's fucking embarrassing. I mean they had an outfielder who didn't have two arms. What's next? Helen Keller pitching.

SQUEAKER: They're in first place. Or at least they were the last time I looked... May 12th, they beat Early Wynn...Now Early Wynn is a great name for a pitcher. Especially if he pitches on opening day.

TRUETT: So they're in first place. They're like the Red Sox. The Red Sox are always in first place in April. It's where you are in October that counts.

SQUEAKER: It's June 6th already. Not April.

TRUETT: I know the date. I'm cold. I'm wet. I'm freezing. I pissed all over myself. So it must be April. Smells like April. (*Sings*) April in Paris.

SQUEAKER: I don't want to go to Paris.

TRUETT: Why not? Once we liberate Paris, the women will be all over us. We'll have to beat them off with a stick.

SQUEAKER: The Frogs don't have no interest in baseball either.

TRUETT: For God's sakes, not everything in life is baseball. There are more important things.

SQUEAKER: Why should there be more important things? If I were God, I'd decree that baseball would be the most important thing ever.

TRUETT: If you were God, Atheism would be the national religion.

SQUEAKER: I don't think there's a day that goes by that I don't think about baseball.

TRUETT: So where does it get you? You're just thinking of ways to pass the time. War, Bridge, Chess, Checkers, Going to the Movies, Getting Laid, Reading the Nespaper, Listening to Abbott and Costello...Just ways to pass the time. Golf... especially golf.

SQUEAKER: I don't play golf.

TRUETT: Well, you should. It would take your mind off baseball and make you concentrate on death.

Truett stands up.

SQUEAKER: Where you going?

TRUETT: (*takes out a hand-grenade*) You cover me. I may not be Bob Feller, but I've got a pretty good arm, and I'm getting sick of looking people whose only purpose in life is to try to kill me.

SQUEAKER: No, no. You cover me. I make a smaller target.

TRUETT: Fuck you. You're a St. Louis Browns fan. You've got a death wish.

SQUEAKER: (*tackles Truett's legs and brings him down*) Baseball fans always want to live to see the next season.

TRUETT: You pull me down one more time and I'll kick your teeth in.

SQUEAKER: You New York Yankee Fans are all alike. Violent. How does anybody survive Yankee Stadium?

TRUETT: I'm violent? Look around you. Where have you been for the past four years?

SQUEAKER: Browns are beating out the Yankees this year. A hundred dollars.

TRUETT: You're on, dog breath. Plus every cigarette you can get your hands on. When World Series time rolls around, the Browns are nowhere to be seen.

SQUEAKER: Forget it. You don't have a hundred dollars. And you don't know nothing about baseball.

TRUETT: I don't? Me? I know enough that an outfielder should have two arms.

SQUEAKER: It's not Pete Gray's fault that he doesn't have two arms.

TRUETT: Did I say it was his fault? But he doesn't have to play baseball. He could be a traffic cop. You can always stop traffic with one hand.

SQUEAKER: What about three-fingered Mordecai Brown?

TRUETT: What about him?

SQUEAKER: You wouldn't let him pitch because he didn't have all five fingers?

TRUETT: Sure. He could pitch. He could pitch for the Browns. What do you think they're going to do with all the wounded tonight? They're going to pick them up and ship them to the Browns. Did you ever ask yourself why they have the only uniforms with a Red Cross on them?

We hear a bullet sing. Truett grabs his left shoulder. His hand and fingers become covered with blood.

TRUETT: Shit...

SQUEAKER: (*stands up*) You sons-a-bitches, you can't shoot a man when he's talking baseball!

TRUETT: Sit down.

Truett holds on to Squeaker's pant's leg.

SQUEAKERL: Let go of my leg, you sonuvabitch.

Squeaker pulls out a grenade, and starts to run toward the concrete bunker.

SQUEAKER: See if you can hit this fast ball, you bastards!

Squeaker runs off. We hear a burst of machine gun fire.

TRUETT: (*crawling painfully*) Squeaker!

Then we hear a grenade blast. German voices. Shouts! Then Squeaker, unwounded, crawls back. The two men now lie facing one another.

TRUETT: Okay. okay, you win. The Browns are going to beat the Yankees. (*He fingers his wound. Studies the blood on his hands and uniform...*) Shit.

Curtain.

THE BANQUET

Scene: This play is best staged in the round or on a three-quarter thrust stage, for the setting consists entirely of a banquet table in a state of preparation. Throughout the opening of the play, and even before the first characters make their appearance, caterers, servants, and waiters constantly bustle in and out, carrying trays of hors-d'oeuvres, meats, pies, flowers, more chairs, etc. The more action the better.

In any case, the room where the banquet is to take place should have no windows in it. It might have a fireplace where no fire burns. There is a chandelier overhead, a very costly and ornamental chandelier that is not on. Stage right of the table is a very uncomfortable antique sofa, perhaps of the Napoleonic era. The one entrance is a large and grandiose door, two doors, in fact, like the entrance to a grand ballroom. Dangling from the ceiling, toward stage left of the banquet table is a large gold cord knotted at the end.

As the audience enters the banquet hall, they are given slips of papers or plastic tags which bear numbers on them, numbers such as are often given out at meat markets or delicatessens. All but numbers 8 and 13 are given out. Numbers 8 and 13 are given to two actors who will be seated in the audience.

The time is now. This is very instant.

ANTOINE ROQUET enters. He is a tall thin man with many effeminate characteristics, including a skin so white that one might think he could see through it. He wears a short white coat, tight black pants, and high, shining boots, and he is clearly in charge of the banquet preparations. He strides angrily to the table where there is a large silver bowl of white chrysanthemums.

ROQUET: *(Loudly.)* Who put these here? Who? Who ordered these? *(With the clip-board that he carries, he dashes the beautiful silver bowl of flowers to the floor, and chrysanthemums and water go spilling every which way. WAITERS and MAIDS immediately converge upon the scene to clean everything up. The MAITRE D' enters. A tall, elegant man, slightly gray at the temples, and quite formally dressed. He stands stiffly and resolute. He has been through such tantrums many times before and he has worked in many of the best hotels in Europe.)*

ROQUET: Maxim, did you order these?

MAXIM: *(Calmly.)* No, Sir. Flowers are not my responsibility. Food and good service are my responsibilities. Unless, of course, your guests are planning to eat the flowers and I should hope, sir, that your guests have much better taste than that.

ROQUET: I will have nothing but passion flowers here. Passion flowers. I will not break tradition for any man, no matter who he is. Nothing is too good for my guests. Nothing. Do you understand that, Maxim? Nothing.

MAXIM: I understand, sir.

ROQUET: *(ROQUET snaps his fingers and simultaneously bursts of flash powder and flames go off around the table, while SERVANTS rush in with bowls of passion flowers.)* Now that's more like it. Passiflora of the family Passifloraceae. Much more appropriate. After all, isn't passion the only thing that matters? The only thing that separates the living from the dead. *(Indicates a very good looking MAID.)* You want her, Maxim? You can have her. Passion. *(Walks angrily to the MAID and lifts and rips her skirt. She offers no resistance.)* Show me passion. You can have everything you want, Maxim, provided you serve me well.

MAXIM: Please, sir, calm yourself.

ROQUET: Make love to her here. Isn't that all the rage now?

MAXIM: Sir, give me the guest list so I know how many to provide for.

ROQUET: Of course, Maxim. You're right. You're absolutely right. Our only passion is the banquet. To devour and be devoured. *(Waving the girl away.)* Go. go. *(ROQUET crosses to the table, picks up a glass, examines it for dust. Puts it down, picks up another one. After a pause, in which he regains his composure.)* He's lived a long time. We could have quite a few guests.

MAXIM: We have always known that the number could be infinite.

ROQUET: Of course, the number could be infinite. In theory,

everything is infinite. Imagine an infinite number of guests. What a ridiculous thing to say. Where would we get the chairs? From Ionesco, I suppose. Tell me, would you have some our guests eat standing up? Maybe that's how you were taught to run a banquet, but I wasn't. I'll allow him one guest for every ten years to get things started. No more, No less. I can't have everyone walking in unexpectedly. Did you ever try to make an infinite amount of oyster dip? Have I ever asked you to do such a thing? And don't think I'd have you start such a thing now.

MAXIM: I thought you might have changed your mind after the last banquet, sir.

ROQUET: Change my mind? I never change my mind. That's what makes me what I am. I am not ecumenical as it were. When I say passion, I mean passion. When I say food, I mean food. Not oysters. Not light bulbs. Not anything but what I say. I am not known for being catholic in my tastes, Maxim, or, at least, not overtly so. *(As ROQUET speaks, MAIDS and WAITERS make their reappearance carrying huge trays of sandwiches and salads. ROQUET plucks an egg from a passing tray.)* Delicious, Maxim. Delicious. You're an absolute genius. I'll send the red-head up to your room tonight. *(ROQUET crosses to the long-haired, red-headed MAID whom he has promised to MAXIM.)* Here dear, help yourself to the oysters, or the deviled eggs. They're aphrodisiacs, you know.

RED-HAIRED MAID: Yes, I know.

ROQUET: I thought you would. *(He stands side by side with her and places his left hand down the front of her dress.)* Maxim has his eye out for you, did you know that?

RED-HAIRED MAID: He's an old man. Aren't there any younger men for me?

ROQUET: It can't be helped, my sweet.

RED-HAIRED MAID: I better have plenty of oysters then.

ROQUET: By all means, help yourself. *(Removes his hand and sniffs the perfume.)*

RED-HAIRED MAID: I prefer you to Maxim.

127

ROQUET: Of course. Who doesn't. That's what makes me what I am.

During the conversation with the MAID, an old man has wandered into the room. He is dressed in a heavy black overcoat, under which he wears formal dinner attire. In his hands, he carries a black hat. He is JEAN-PAUL with a mass of uncombed hair, and watery blue eyes. He wears glasses that have no discernible frames. It is easy to sense that we are in the presence of a very intellectual man.

JEAN-PAUL: Pardon me, is this where the….

ROQUET: *(Noticing the man for the first time.)* Are you the violinist? It's about time. I don't know why it takes so long to get one of you people down here, and don't bother with any long-winded excuses about the union. You can hang your things up over there. *(Indicating a single clothes-stand.)* And you can start right away. Nothing too fancy. Just some simple love songs. Do you know "Some of These Days?" I believe it is one of his favorites.

JEAN-PAUL: But I'm not the violinist…

ROQUET: *(Continuing without listening.)* Actually, if you get a request from the guests, play it. Music to suit the guests. Can you play philosophically…? What did you say?

JEAN-PAUL: But I'm not the violinist.

ROQUET: You're not the violinist. Goddamn it. What do you play? The clarinet? We have so many clarinet players down here you wouldn't believe it. I ask for a violinist and they send me a clarinetist. Last time they sent me a hare lipped man on the bassoon. Ever see a hare lipped bassoonist? Absolutely ridiculous, darling.

JEAN-PAUL: But I don't play anything. I'm Jean-Paul.

ROQUET: Jean-Paul! Monsieur. Excusez-moi. *(Embracing him.)* I should have known right away, of course. Oh, this is so very embarrassing. After all, I've been planning this banquet for a long time. My, how you've changed. Overnight as it were. You didn't look like that at all….Oh, it is immensely stupid of me. But you see, we've had so many banquets lately. *(Taking his hand.)* Salve!

JEAN-PAUL: This is the right place then. I didn't really believe I would get lost.

ROQUET: Of course, Jean-Paul. You didn't expect to go anywhere else, did you?

JEAN-PAUL: The invitation did say your place. *(Smiling gently).* You do take credit cards, don't you?

ROQUET: No, here, people pay and through the teeth. But the music, the music. How can we have a banquet without music. *(Calling to MAXIM.)* Maxim, get the damned violinist here, will you.

MAXIM: Do people eat music? Then that is not my area of jurisdiction.

ROQUET: Don't get temperamental with me, Maxim, or heads will roll. I said get a violinist here. I don't care who he is provided he can play something with love, love, love in it. *(To JEAN-PAUL.)* You do like love, don't you?

JEAN-PAUL: Like love? A strange question. At my age...

ROQUET: Bah, humbug. Look at Maxim. He's a lot older than you, and look at the hot little piece he's got lined up with him...with my help, of course.

JEAN-PAUL: Why, of course.

ROQUET: And some aphrodisiacs. The oysters are very fine. The oyster and the carpenter. It wasn't the oyster and the carpenter, was it?

JEAN-PAUL: Well, I know what to expect. Can't we simply get on to the ordeal?

ROQUET: Ordeal?

JEAN-PAUL: Excuse me. I didn't quite mean it that way.

ROQUET: No, of course not. *(Bitchy.)* And you do know what to expect, don't you?

JEAN-PAUL: *(Removing his coat and placing it over the sofa.)* Well, naturally, I have my ideas.

129

ROQUET: Naturally. *(Angrily.)* And hang up your coat, darling. This is not an outhouse. There's a place for everything here. *(Grabs the coat from the sofa and hangs it on the coat-stand).* Don't expect me to do everything for you here.

JEAN-PAUL: *(Politely.)* Thank you.

ROQUET: No need to thank me. I have plenty of surprises in store for you.

JEAN-PAUL: Please, I'm too old for surprises.

ROQUET: Not the surprises of Antoine Roquet. If people knew what to expect, it would be hardly necessary to go through all of this trouble. *(Passing a tray of hors-d'oeuvres.)* Oysters and crackers? Most people think it is the oysters that are the aphrodisiac, but it is actually the crackers. See, I'm not entirely devoid of humor as you might have been led to expect.

JEAN-PAUL: Thank you, but I'll wait for the others.

ROQUET: Then you are expecting others.

JEAN-PAUL: It is the definition of a banquet, isn't it?

ROQUET: Oh you and your definitions. It is enough to bring on nausea. How do you know that I'm not playing a joke on you? I do have a wicked sense of humor, you know. Suppose I say that nobody is expected to show up.

JEAN-PAUL: I expect you to say that to fool me and then to surprise me with guests.

ROQUET: You think that! I say no guests are coming because you believe I never tell the truth. The old Father of Lies bit. Hence, you expect the opposite of what I say to be true. Since you expect the opposite, I tell you the truth. Reverse psychology. I am not as transparent as you think.

JEAN-PAUL: Then I reverse your reverse psychology. I tell you that I expect guests when I don't expect guests so you will surprise me by inviting guests.

ROQUET: But, darling, I know that's what you expect. You don't really believe that I will fulfill your expectations, do you? Hence, I

130

am going to surprise you by giving you what you expect.

JEAN-PAUL: Giving me what I expect will definitely be s surprise.

ROQUET: Yes. Well then we shall see what we shall see. Nihil est sine culpa.

JEAN-PAUL: Latin, monsieur!

ROQUET: I always try to keep up with the Pope. I feel it is one of my duties.

JEAN-PAUL: Somehow I cannot picture you with duties.

ROQUET: Well I do have duties. And one of them is to get some information for my files. *(Looks at his clip board.)* Year of birth?

JEAN-PAUL: Is this really necessary? I thought you would have all the information by now?

ROQUET: *(Peevishly.)* You think, you think, you think, but you do not know. You don't know a thing.

JEAN-PAUL: Then I know I do not know.

ROQUET: No, you don't even know that. And don't play games with me. I've had the Socrates crap up to here. *(His hand above his head.)* You should have seen his banquet. Alcibiades putting it up the old rectum.

JEAN-PAUL: Please....

ROQUET: Then don't ruin this get acquainted session. I have too much to do to keep track of everybody. Besides, we've had a number of impersonators lately.

JEAN-PAUL: And who would impersonate me?

ROQUET: People have ways of impersonating themselves. Date of birth?

JEAN-PAUL: June 21, 1905.

ROQUET: Cancer. *(The astrological sign is flashed onto the ceiling.)* Cancers are such fun. Cancer, you know, symbolizes tenacity, the ability of the reflective mind to hold on stubbornly to an idea.

JEAN-PAUL: Astrological rubbish!

ROQUET: *(Stamping his foot.)* Not here!

JEAN-PAUL: *(Mockingly.)* Then what sign were you born under?

ROQUET: I was born under them all, and I share all their characteristics.

JEAN-PAUL: I should have thought you were a Gemini. You do have all the characteristics.

ROQUET: Who is analyzing whom here? Parents?

JEAN-PAUL: I have parents, if that is what you mean?

ROQUET: You know what I mean. I trust you to know about meaning.

JEAN-PAUL: Suppose I say I have no father. Will that make you jealous?

ROQUET: Make me jealous? Now what would give you that idea?

JEAN-PAUL: Because you have a father and I have none. Hence, I have no need to prove my power to anyone. No old man to destroy to win my mother's affection. The way you bellow out commands.

ROQUET: I do not bellow. I am not in the habit of bellowing.

JEAN-PAUL: Giving orders then. The way you give commands to prove yourself. I have absolutely no desire for such a position.

ROQUET: We'll see. Maxim! Where is that demned vilinist?

MAXIM enters with his staff. He carries a sheaf of papers and is involved with making last-minute check on the state of the dining table. As MAXIM goes through his check-list of preparations, ROQUET continues with his questioning.

MAXIM: Yes, yes. I'm taking care of it. There are just so many good ones to choose from. Staff, let's make sure that everything is absolutely perfect before the rest arrive.

JEAN-PAUL: He did say 'the rest."

ROQUET: Pay no attention to him. I have the final say…in everything. Now about your parents. Your father.

The following conversations take place simultaneously.

JEAN-PAUL: He died when I was young.

MAXIM: Deviled eggs. Check. Hence no father.

ROQUET: And so?

MAXIM: Champagne. 1864. Check.

JEAN-PAUL: And so I was raised by Uncle Charles. MAXIM: Oysters. Check. Crackers. Check.

ROQUET: Charles Schweitzer?

MAXIM: Olives. Check. Cheese. Check.

JEAN-PAUL: You know of him? *(No response from ROQUET.)*

MAXIM: Fingerbowls. Check. Yes, an uncle of Albert's.

ROQUET: *(Sarcastically.)* Ah yes. Dear dear.

MAXIM: Napkins. Check. *(Picks one up and unfolds it.)* Albert. I had so wanted to meet him. A saint. Why isn't this a veritable saint monogrammed? Take it back. *(tosses it to one of the WAITRESSES.)*

JEAN-PAUL: Can't entertain everyone you wish, I imagine.

MAXIM: Now to check the settings for initial party.

ROQUET: Eo tempore non poteram id facere. But we are indeed fortunate to have gotten you.

MAXIM: 6 complete place settings. Each consisting of 3 foks, 2 spoons, 2 knives, cups, saucers, water glass...

JEAN-PAUL: Charmed, I'm sure.

ROQUET: Education?

MAXIM: There's a knife missing. That's impossible. It was here earlier.

JEAN-PAUL: Graduated from the ecole Normale superieure in...oh I don't know. It's been so long ago. Somebody has taken one of the sterling silver knives.

ROQUET: Try 1929.

MAXIM: *(To one of the MALE WAITERS)*: You give me that knife. I saw you take it. You're not goint to get away with it, do you understand? You thought you'd steal it, did you? You think we have no morals here? Now where were we? We were getting the school out of your system. Or were we getting your system out of

JEAN-PAUL: All right. 1929. It sounds right.

ROQUET: Maxim, goddamn it. Will you keep the noise down? I can hardly hear myself think.

RED-HAIRED MAID: He's new here, your schools? Maxim.

JEAN-PAUL: If you knew me better, you would know that I have no system.

MAXIM: Shut up, bitch. You're always ready to protect anything in pants. As long as they have a tool for you to play with.

ROQUET: I was merely making a jest, darling. Puns are my favorite form of humor.

WAITER: *(Obviously nervous and frightened.)* No, sir. You've got me all wrong. I wasn't trying to steal the knife. I had noticed it was dirty, that's all. Look at it yourself. *(Tosses the knife onto the table.)* Look at it. It's filthy. I was going to take it back to the kitchen, that's all. I was just taking it back to the kitchen.

JEAN-PAUL: The lowest form of humor.

ROQUET: Appropriate for me then?

JEAN-PAUL: Comme ci, commac ca....

ROQUET: I am a master of language , you know. It is the chief instrument in my work.

MAXIM: And who told you to do it?

(Off-stage we can hear Hitler giving a speech to his troops and the steady rhythm of goose-stepping soldiers marching through the streets. The sound is up.)

WAITER: I'm new here. I haven't worked many of these

banquets.

ROQUET: Let's see now. In World War II, you were captured by the Germans, but you escaped and became a leader in the resistance movement.

MAXIM: Go to your room. You won't be working many more when we get through why do you ask? Are you trying to wear me down through one absurdity after another? *(The sounds fade away.)*

JEAN-PAUL: If you know all about me, it's like confession. It's simply for your own good.

RED-HAIRED MAID: *(Shouts at MAXIM.)* Beast!

ROQUET: Les mots, les mots. Or in Latin of the Black Mass: Verbi, verbi. Words, words. *(MAXIM slaps the MAID.)*

WAITER: Forgive me, sir. Please, forgive me. I didn't mean it.

JEAN-PAUL: Your consideration astonishes.

MAXIM: *Forgive?* Where did you ever get a word like that?

ROQUET: It shouldn't. I'm a selfish individual.

WAITER: What in the hell was I going to do with a knife anyway. A lot good a knife is going to do me...I always put other people first. Anyway, I thought that you being a Cancer would know what it is like to be lousy always thought to be egotistical and vain. Human life, as you say, starts on the other side of despair, and so naturally everybody puts himself first. His she? *(Indicating the RED-HAIRED MAID.)*

MAXIM: She put you up to it, didn't freedom...

JEAN-PAUL: You've read my books. I take it.

WAITER: No. She had nothing to do with it..

ROQUET: No, no, no. Don't leap to conclusions, darling. Outline guides are available to me too. Or on top of that what she you'd put one over on old Maxim. Isn't that told you?

MAXIM: She said she'd lay for you if conversations with other fellow guests. I should like to have read everything you have written, that intellectual vomit of yours, but you know how it is.

WAITER: No. *(He tries to run but two other SERVANTS grab him and hold him. They bring him to his knees.)* I really just know have the time.

JEAN-PAUL: I thought that if you had anything at all, it would be time.

MAXIM: She said all you had to do was prove your manhood and she would provide a place for you to put it.

ROQUET: Time, time.

WAITER: No. It's only a lousy knife for God's sake, and it isn't even yours. The Piper's son stole a world. And away he run....Political categories?

MAXIM: For whose sake? *(The* affiliations? *WAITER is silent.)* Take him away. *(The WAITER is dragged off. MAXIM picks up examines it, wipes it on his sleeve, and carefully places it on the table in its proper place.)* There is a result. Chaos would rear its ugly head everything. If there weren't, chaos dragging the whole universe down with it....Now about the like a great steed doesn't have an eraser on it.

JEAN-PAUL: Do you want nice neat place for   *the knife, holds it up,*

ROQUET: Do the best you can, but don't contradict yourself. As you can see, my pencil would tonight.

JEAN-PAUL: Well how about Republican ass Democrat. Will that do? I want the women to show plenty of

ROQUET: Your party folded in 52. That just goes to show what's wrong with you. How little serve a banquet, I can't sit down for a week?

WAITRESS: How come every time I you know yourself. One contradiction after another. Will somebody tell me that? Why do men pinch all the time for? What's it prove? *(Scoffing.)* Republican-Democrat. To unravel the have to meaning of those terms would turn a saint into a semanticist. You write and you write and you

MAXIM: At the very least, it proves you write, and all you're really concerned with is that have a pretty ass. Besides it helps the men someday you're going to die and that the devil is to work up an appetite, and thus they going to screw your ass to the wall. Appreciate the food better. Tonight, my dear, you will be serving refined men, so maybe usual proddings and pinchings.

JEAN-PAUL: Oh, is that what you're your ample exterior posterior will be spared its going to do to me? I'm going to turn my back to the devil prick?

ROQUET: I'm sorry. I shouldn't have brought anything.

WAITRESS: Refined men, my ass. They're the worse of the bunch, because they think they're doing you a favor rolling a bit of your backside between their thumb and forefinger. *(There's a knock at the door.)* Roquet: Maxim, get the door will? I think a guest has arrived.

MAXIM: Do people eat doors?

ROQUET: *(Heavy sarcasm.)* I know. It's not your jurisdiction.

JEAN-PAUL: I really would like to wash up before greeting the others. *(MAXIM crosses to the door.)*

MAXIM: *(To ROQUET.)* Everything is set.

ROQUET: *(To JEAN-PAUL.)* Why are your hands dirty? *(To MAXIM.)* Wait, I'll get the door myself. I've changed my mind.

WAITRESS: *(Removing her panties under her skirt.)* I feel so indecent without any underthings on.

MATHIEU, A WAITER: What's a girl like you doing in a place like this?

WAITRESS: Shove it. You hear me. You're not any better than me, and you better remember that. Do you hear me? You're not better than me. Neither is the old guy there.

JEAN-PAUL: Please, miss. I never claimed anything of the kind.

WAITRESS: That's o.k., pops. I'm just nervous, that's all. *(There is the sound of a train going by. A loud whistling chugging train. A SMALL BOY, aged eight, walks forward with ROQUET to shake hands with*

JEAN-PAUL. He is dressed in short pants and he carries a book satchel. He is dressed in the French fashions of 1913.)

ROQUET: Jean-Paul, allow me to introduce you to your first guest - Jean-Paul meet Jean-Paul.

JEAN-PAUL: Ah what a coincidence that we have the same name, young man.

JEAN-PAUL (8): Pleased to meet you, monsieur. *(To ROQUET.)* Where's the bathroom?

JEAN-PAUL: Funny, I was asking the same thing, myself. My hair is mussed up, and I'd like to wash my hands. I'm sure that I do not look like a guest of honor.

ROQUET: I'm afraid there are no washrooms available on this level.

JEAN-PAUL: Upstairs then?

ROQUET: Upstairs? *(Off-stage is the sound of wind, birds. This is under the next seven lines of dialogue and then out.)*

JEAN-PAUL: *(Realizing that there is to be no answer from ROQUET.)* A mirror would help.

ROQUET: A mirror? I thought you knew better than that. There are no mirrors here.

JEAN-PAUL: How foolish of me to expect otherwise.

ROQUET: In spite of everything, people still expect mirrors.

JEAN-PAUL (8): I'm going to wet my pants.

ROQUET: No, you won't. No fear of that.

JEAN-PAUL (8): May I sit down then?

JEAN-PAUL: By all means, young man with my name. You may even sit at the head of the table if you wish. After all, I am in no mood to be gaped at by strangers.

ROQUET: *(Vehemently.)* No! He can sit anywhere he wants to but not at the head of the table. That is for the guest of honor.
(Without speaking. JEAN-PAUL (8) goes to the table and takes one of the

138

chairs. He places his satchel on the table and begins to spread his books and papers out before him. Off-stage there is the distant sound of a train passing into the night.)

JEAN-PAUL: Somehow I didn't expect my guests to be so young.

ROQUET: The surprises of Antoine Roquet.

JEAN-PAUL: Are they all to be so young? Is that to be your feeble-minded joke?

ROQUET: Is he so young?

JEAN-PAUL: Why he can't be more than nine or ten.

ROQUET: Maybe he's a midget, darling. Don't leap to conclusions.

JEAN-PAUL: Without a wrinkle on him.

ROQUET: He is old as you, Jean-Paul.

JEAN-PAUL: I thank you for the compliment. I wish I felt that young. I know I don't feel that young. How old are you, Jean-Paul?

JEAN-PAUL (8): Eight and a half.

JEAN-PAUL: Good for you. By the time I was your age, I had seen death straight in the face, climbing up over the balcony, staring through the bay windows, its great hulk of a nose pressed against the glass.

JEAN-PAUL (8): I have seen death, monsieur.

JEAN-PAUL: Why then, we have a lot in common.

JEAN-PAUL (8): *(To ROQUET.)* If I could have some light, I could do my homework.

ROQUET: Sorry, the chandelier is for decorative purposes only. It doesn't work. Well, I will leave you two to get acquainted. I have some things to attend to in the kitchen, but I shall be right back. Running a banquet requires a lot of planning, you know.

JEAN-PAUL: Of course...*(ROQUET claps his hands and all of the remaining SERVANTS exit, leaving behind the banquet table completely furnished, standing in a dimly lit room. ROQUET exits, and a great, heavy door clangs shut. JEAN-PAUL crosses to where the young boy is sitting.)*

JEAN-PAUL: Did you enjoy your train ride?

JEAN-PAUL (8): What train ride?

JEAN-PAUL: Oh, didn't you come by train?

JEAN-PAUL (8): No.

JEAN-PAUL: I thought I had heard a train...If you wish. I'll light some of these candles for you. When I was your age, I used to do my readings by candlelight.

JEAN-PAUL (8): Thank you, monsieur.

JEAN-PAUL: *(Lights three candles on the table and places them near the boy.)* What subjects are you studying? Maybe I can help you. I was a teacher once.

JEAN-PAUL (8): What did you teach?

JEAN-PAUL: Philosophy.

JEAN-PAUL (8): I don't have philosophy.

JEAN-PAUL: Oh.

JEAN-PAUL (8): Actually, I'm writing a story.

JEAN-PAUL: Really?

JEAN-PAUL (8): It's about the city and the black death.

JEAN-PAUL: I should like to read it when you're done. I've done some writing myself...Is my tie straight?

JEAN-PAUL (8):   Yes, monsieur.

JEAN-PAUL: What do your parents think about your writing?

JEAN-PAUL (8): I don't know. Besides my father's dead.

JEAN-PAUL: I'm sorry to hear that. Well maybe someday I'll be able to tell my friends how a famous author came to my banquet.

JEAN-PAUL (8): I hope so, monsieur.

JEAN-PAUL: My friends all call me Jean. Why don't you call me Jean?

JEAN-PAUL (8): I don't have any friends.

JEAN-PAUL: No? None at all?

JEAN-PAUL (8): I'm ugly.

JEAN-PAUL: Come now. You must be jesting. You're going to be the most handsome fellow at my banquet.

JEAN-PAUL (8): I don't care. I'm going to be a great author and then everybody'll be sorry they weren't my friend.

JEAN-PAUL: Why I'm sure they are sorry now. But you're too young, too handsome, too talented to be alone. Why in a few years the women will be flocking around you.

JEAN-PAUL (8): I don't like girls.

JEAN-PAUL: I was once that way myself, but you'll change. We're like the crab on the ceiling. We go forwards and backwards.

JEAN-PAUL (8): No. I'll never change.

JEAN-PAUL: Parcelus would agree with you, but not Heraclitus. You won't believe me, but twenty years from now, you won't be able to recognize yourself.

JEAN-PAUL (8): How do you spell *transcendentalism?*

JEAN-PAUL: *Transcendentalism?*

JEAN-PAUL (8): I want to put it into my story. The knight was a student of transcendentalism.

JEAN-PAUL: Such big words. You must go to a very fine school. T-R-A-N-S-C-E-N-D-E-N-T-A-L-I-S-M. Spelling. I don't think I knew such big words at your age. *(Off-stage can be heard sounds of the sea and a large boat sailing.)* But how does one recognize genius? *(He recites.)*

> *Comme je descendais des Fleuves impossibles,*
>
> *Je ne me sentis guide par les haleurs:*
>
> *Des Peaux-Rouge criards les avaient pris pour cibles,*
>
> *Les ayant cloues nus eux poteaux de couleurs.*

Roquet was right, Jean. We're both the same age, both writing about transcendental knights. Perhaps, like Rimbaud, I should have quit at nineteen. *(ROQUET enters through the audience, leading five gentlemen who follow in orderly fashion. They are dressed in different fashions of the various decades of the twentieth century. JEAN-PAUL (38) is dressed in a military uniform.)*

ROQUET: Gentlemen, right this way, please.

JEAN-PAUL: Aha, Jean, our guests are arriving. And didn't I tell you that you'd be the most handsome of the lot?

ROQUET: Jean-Paul, your guests. *(The guests bow politely at the waist. JEAN-PAUL looks at them quizzically...)*

JEAN-PAUL: But, Monsieur Roquet, who are these men?

ROQUET: Don't tell me that I've surprised you once again, Jean-Paul!

JEAN-PAUL: I definitely did not expect racks and whips, if that's what you mean.

ROQUET: Don't fool yourself. They may well exist...*(Screams and remarks are heard off-stage from the servant who was caught stealing the knife.)*

WAITER: I didn't steal the knife....

RED-HAIRED MAID: Leave him alone, will you?

CROQUET: Maxim, close those damned doors will you? I'm carrying on a civilized conversation with our guest of honor.

WAITER: *(In great agony.)* Aaaah! *(Huge doors can be heard slamming shut. And then an echo. And then another echo. The sounds of a fire-engine roaring through the streets. Sirens.)*

JEAN-PAUL: *(Matter-of-factly.)* The servant with the knife. Such a great fuss over such a slight object.

ROQUET: Homo de quo dicebas est stultus. It is a shame that they are taking Latin off college diplomas.

JEAN-PAUL (18): A dead language.

ROQUET: In the mind of a fool, all languages are dead....Oh, who lit the candles?

142

JEAN-PAUL: I did. I wanted my friend here to have light to read by.

ROQUET: Not at all necessary for you to stoop to such a thing. We have servants for that sort of thing. And there is a light. *(ROQUET claps his hands and the great chandelier overhead goes on.)*

JEAN-PAUL: *(Surprised.)* You lied. Jean, Monsieur Roquet lied to us. The chandelier works.

ROQUET: *(To JEAN-PAUL.)* I'm surprised at you. You mean to stand there and say that you did not expect me to lie? Oculi nostri sine cura non valebunt.

JEAN-PAUL: But to lie about such a trivial thing when the boy wanted to write....It's so....so...

ROQUET: Absurd?

JEAN-PAUL: If you like.

ROQUET: No, not if I like. There are, after all, other words. Malicious. Evil.

JEAN-PAUL: Bah, don't flatter yourself. You are not capable of evil.

ROQUET: I am not capable of evil?

JEAN-PAUL: No. You are not capable of evil. *(He feels a sharp pain and grimaces.)*

JEAN-PAUL (38): Pardon me, gentlemen, but it has been a long trip for all of us. I was wondering if we might sit down and have something to drink.

ROQUET: Oh by all means. Please forgive my rudeness. Just choose wherever you would like to sit, but please remember that the guest of honor is at the table's head.

JEAN-PAUL (38): *(Bowing slightly at the waist.)* Why, of course, Monsieur.

ROQUET: *(Angrily.)* Choose. Choose your places. *(Sardonically.)* Gentlemen, my sweets, my darlings.

JEAN-PAUL: *(In an uncommon outbursts.)* Roquet, I won't have my

143

guests treated so.

ROQUET: *(Caught off-guard.)* So much passion in a teacher of philosophy. One might expect it in poets or suffragettes, but not in a man concerned with objectivity. Feelings get in the way...Gentlemen, please be seated. I humbly apologize for this outbursts from our guest of honor, but honor has a way of going to a man's head. If you should want anything, simply pull the bell cord, and Maxim or myself will see to your wishes. Now we will see if I am capable of evil. *(ROQUET takes out a pair of glasses and puts them on to read something from a small slip of paper taken out of the pocket of his jacket.)* Number eight. Is there a number eight out there? *(A short pause. A man in the audience with the number eight stands up with the slip in his hand.)*

MAN IN AUDIENCE: I...I have it.

ROQUET: Good, come with me, please. *(Bowing slightly to the men at the banquet table.)*

MAN IN AUDIENCE: But what about my wife?

ROQUET: Does she have number eight?

MAN IN AUDIENCE: No.

ROQUET: Then just you. Come along.

MAN IN AUDIENCE: But this is ridiculous. I don't want to.

ROQUET: I'm afraid you have no choice, unless you want us to use force.

MAN IN AUDIENCE: But I paid money. *(Making his way out of the audience, acquiescing to ROQUET'S powers.)* I didn't expect anything like this. I just came to watch like the rest.

ROQUET: I'm sure you will enjoy what we have in store for you much more than the banquet.

MAN IN AUDIENCE: *(Following ROQUET out.)* But I want to see it. *(ROQUET and the MAN exit. A huge door can be heard shutting and then the echo of the door and then another echo.)*

JEAN-PAUL: You're wrong, Roquet. The word you want is

diabolical, not absurd, not evil. *(He clutches at his heart. He is in obvious pain.)* Oh, damn it. *(JEAN-PAUL (18) and JEAN-PAUL (28) come to his aid and help him to the antique, uncomfortable sofa.)*

JEAN-PAUL (18): Here, old man, lie down awhile. You'll be all right.

JEAN-PAUL: All right? What a laugh! I died today. *(JEAN-PAUL (8) brings the philosopher a glass of water.)* That's good of you, Jean. I'm afraid you're not going to get much writing done tonight...Did I tell you all that we have a famous writer in our midst....permit me to introduce you all to Jean-Paul, author of The City and The Black Plague.

JEAN-PAUL (8): The real title is the *Transcendental Knight.*

JEAN-PAUL: Ah yes, that's the real title.

JEAN-PAUL (28): Let me undo your tie, old man.

JEAN-PAUL: And after I went to all the trouble of straightening it out.

JEAN-PAUL (18): You're going to be all right....Just try to relax awhile.

JEAN-PAUL: Gentlemen, I'm sorry, but I don't believe I heard your names. I only know Jean here.

JEAN-PAUL (18): You mean the old guy doesn't know?

JEAN-PAUL (48): Roquet probably didn't get around to telling him.

JEAN-PAUL: Are you all writers too? Teachers? Men just chosen at random?

JEAN-PAUL (58): In a sense, I suppose, you might call us all writers.

JEAN-PAUL: I had no idea that this was going to be such a literary banquet. Keep sharp, Jean. You might make some very important contacts tonight.

JEAN-PAUL (18): But which Jean are you talking to?

JEAN-PAUL: Why to him, of course. *(Indicates young JEAN.)*

JEAN-PAUL (28): Why *of course?* My name is Jean too.

JEAN-PAUL (18): And mine too.

JEAN-PAUL (58): And mine too.

JEAN-PAUL: Maybe it's Roquet's way of ordering things. But the last name...

JEAN-PAUL (48): But don't you understand? We're all Jean-Paul's. All the names are the same...we are the same ....

JEAN-PAUL: What's Roquet trying to pull anyway?

JEAN-PAUL (18): Who cares as long as the company is good?

JEAN-PAUL (28): And the champagne...Where the wine is good and the people, then all is well. Who could ask for anything more...A round for everyone *(Opens a bottle of champagne and begins to pour.)*....

JEAN-PAUL: You shouldn't have to do that. Roquet said that there are servants for everything.

JEAN-PAUL (58): Pull the bell-cord.

JEAN-PAUL: It probably doesn't work. It is the kind of hoax I would suspect from Roquet.

JEAN-PAUL (18): To hell with all servants; we serve ourselves. *(JEAN-PAUL (38) pulls the bell cord.)*

JEAN-PAUL (58): A toast:

> *Je sucerai, pour noyer ma rancoeur,*
>
> *Le Nepenthes et la bonne cigue*
>
> *Aux bouts charmants de cette gorge aigue*
>
> *Qui n'a jamais emprisonne de couer....*

JEAN-PAUL (48): A strange toast from Baudelaire...

JEAN-PAUL (58): So what does it matter? I've had my say about him, and it sprang to mind.

JEAN-PAUL (38): But what about little Jean? Should we ask for something else for him?

JEAN-PAUL (8): I'm not little.

JEAN-PAUL (38): Of course not. I didn't mean it that way....

JEAN-PAUL: This is his banquet too. Champagne for all...

JEAN-PAUL (18): But not the toast from Baudelaire. *(He pours champagne to the top of his glass and steps to the top of the table.)*

JEAN-PAUL (58): Why what's wrong with it?

JEAN-PAUL (28): Do you really mean that stuff about having no heart confined within your breast?

JEAN-PAUL (58): A heart, a heart. We should all be like crabs scuttling on the floor of the ocean, skittling here, skittling there...

JEAN-PAUL (18): To Simone.

JEAN-PAUL: Ah Simone, does anybody know how she is?

JEAN-PAUL (18): Beautiful and young. That is what matters. None of this "Qui n'a jamais emprisonne de couer."

JEAN-PAUL: Young? *(Momentarily puzzled.)* Yes, of course, young. But why have you chosen to toast my Simone. Surely you have someone of your own to dedicate a toast to.

JEAN-PAUL (18): *Your* Simone! *My* Simone!

JEAN-PAUL (28): No, my Simone.

JEAN-PAUL (38): No, our Simone.

JEAN-PAUL (58): No, she is Simone for all of us.

JEAN-PAUL (8): I don't know anybody named Simone.

JEAN-PAUL (18): Ah but you will. You will....*(MAXIM enters. We can hear in the distance strains of circus music.)*

MAXIM: The bell cord was pulled.

JEAN-PAUL (58): Some time ago.

JEAN-PAUL (28): No, not too long ago.

JEAN-PAUL (18): We should like to be served. Before we all get crocked.

JEAN-PAUL (8): I won't get crocked. I like champagne.

MAXIM: Monsieur Roquet thought that you might like some time to recover from your journey before being served. He thought you might like to get acquainted.

JEAN-PAUL (58): I am afraid we are all too well acquainted.

MAXIM: Well, isn't that marvelous? I am so glad that everything is turning out so well. *(Two male SERVANTS make their appearance in the audience and walk slowly down to where number 13 is seated. Outside the door, there are the sounds of a carnival. Rides, music, people, the side-show laughter.)*

JEAN-PAUL (38): I compliment you on your champagne. I realize that with a war on it must be extremely difficult to run an efficient banquet.

MAXIM: Monsieur Roquet does the best he can. It is what makes him what he is.

JEAN-PAUL (18): War? What war?

JEAN-PAUL (28): Yes, monsieur, what war?

JEAN-PAUL (38): The World War, of course.

JEAN-PAUL (18): Why that was over years ago.

JEAN-PAUL (58): I should have thought you were talking about Viet-Nam.

JEAN-PAUL (39): Viet-Nam? Never heard of it. Why right at this moment France is being butchered by Hitler and his...

JEAN-PAUL (28): Butchering France? Who is butchering France?

JEAN-PAUL (58): France is butchering herself in Viet-Nam, as she butchered herself in Algiers. The whole world is in revolt.

JEAN-PAUL (38): No, no, no. I'm talking about the Germans of course.

JEAN-PAUL (18): Please, you're jesting. The Germans surrendered.

JEAN-PAUL (38): Surrendered? When was that? It must have been quite recently for I've had no news. I was captured by the Germans and made my escape. I am back now to work for the

Resistance.

JEAN-PAUL (18): The Resistance? All you are resisting is making sense.

MAXIM: Gentlemen, gentlemen, don't you see that you are talking at cross-purposes. You'll never get anywhere this way.

JEAN-PAUL (58): If we don't get anywhere now, we'll never get anywhere. A man has got to begin somewhere.

MAXIM: What a foolish time to talk about beginnings. Well, I'll let Roquet explain it to you. *(Looks at the slip of paper in his hand.)* Ah, what a coincidence. Unlucky thirteen. Will number thirteen come with me, please? Number thirteen! *(A slight pause. No one in the audience admits that he has number thirteen.)* Please, ladies and gentlemen, please co-operate. We do have forever so waiting is no object. It would simply be courteous on your part. While waiting you have been allowed to watch the philosopher's banquet out of the goodness of Roquet's heart, and do not think there is no goodness there, for it is primarily goodness that inspires his revolt. There is only one evil, as Jean-Paul will tell you, and that is the irreducibility of man and the world of Thought. So it does you no good to be afraid. If number thirteen, whoever holds number thirteen, would come forward.

MATHIEU, THE WAITER: Here it is, Maxim. I saw it. I saw it. The woman here has it. She's trying to destroy the slip. *(The two WAITERS surround a woman in the audience. She is in her late twenties, quite attractive, and dressed in a dark skirt and blouse.)*

NUMBER THIRTEEN: No. No. I don't have it. It's a mistake. Leave me alone.

WAITER NO. 2, BRUNET: No, it's no mistake, lady. *(He grabs the woman's wrist and twists it.)*

NUMBER THIRTEEN: Stop it, you're hurting me. *(She drops the paper.)*

MATHIEU, THE WAITER: *(Bending over to pick up the paper.)* Here it is. Number thirteen. Just as we said.

NUMBER THIRTEEN: Get away from me. You can't treat me like this.

MAXIM: Who says we can't? We are the sole judge of things here, not you.

NUMBER THIRTEEN: I came to watch...like the man...Where is number eight? What did you do to him? *(Hysterically.)* Leave me alone. I don't want to die.

MAXIM: Who said anything about dying? I don't recall anybody even mentioning it.

MATHIEU, THE WAITER: *(Slapping the woman.)* The bitch bit me.

MAXIM: This will not go good with you. If there is one thing Roquet appreciates, it is co-operation. *(The WAITERS carry the woman toward the door.)*

NUMBER THIRTEEN: You're crazy. All of you are crazy. You can't just sit here and let them take me away.

MAXIM: There's a banquet, a beautiful banquet waiting for you. Who could ask for anything more?

MATHIEU, THE WAITER: Open the door.

BRUNET, THE WAITER: I've got it. *(The woman is carried through the doors by the two WAITERS. As the doors open and close, and the echo of doors closing is heard, the carnival sounds come to an end, and we hear a lone bird singing.)*

MAXIM: *(To Jean-Paul.)* Please excuse the interruption. We had all wanted your banquet to be so very special. The most special of all in fact.

JEAN-PAUL (8): I'm hungry.

JEAN-PAUL (48): Yes, when shall we eat?

MAXIM: But you have hardly touched the hors-d'oeuvres. And my staff and I have spent so much time preparing them. But you will be served soon. You will all be served soon. *(He bows at the waist and exits. As the great doors close, there can be heard the sounds of voices and guns firing in the street.)*

JEANPAUL: Somehow, I should have preferred to be fed in a more natural place.

JEAN-PAUL (48): Are any places natural?

JEAN-PAUL: Well, to dine on the sixth floor of my apartment house in Paris. Now that seems to me to be natural. The sixth floor of any place in Paris. To look down on the streets, and the people out walking, the young people on bicycles, - that would be a natural place.

JEAN-PAUL (28): You must be feeling better, old man.

JEAN-PAUL: Yes, I feel much better, thank you.

JEAN-PAUL (8): And I don't have to go to the bathroom anymore.

JEAN-PAUL: Good for you, Jean. At least Roquet didn't lie about that.

JEAN-PAUL (18): *(Raising his champagne.)* To the old man's health. I'm confident he will outlive us all.

JEAN-PAUL (38): I wish this damn crab over our heads would go. It definitely does not help my appetite.

JEAN-PAUL (48): Its beauty leaves a lot to be desired.

JEAN-PAUL (58): Perhaps if we complained to Roquet about the decor, he would change it.

JEAN-PAUL (28): In that case, I'll ring for him.

JEAN-PAUL (8): No, let me. I want to pull the cord.

JEAN-PAUL (28): Of course, Jean. Let me help you. *(He picks JEAN up by the waist so that the boy can reach the bell cord. When young JEAN tugs at the bell cord, it comes off into his hands.)*

JEAN-PAUL (58): What did you do, Jean? You pulled the cord too hard.

JEAN-PAUL: No, it's just another one of Roquet's tricks. That cord was never designed to work.

151

JEAN-PAUL (18): It worked before when we called Maxim.

JEAN-PAUL: He might well have come anyway.

JEAN-PAUL (38): Don't tell me that you're going to argue against cause and effect. You lay a girl and she gets pregnant and you say it might well have happened anyway.

JEAN-PAUL (28): Well, let's not discount virgin births.

JEAN-PAUL: Please, not in front of young Jean.

JEAN-PAUL (8): I know all about it.

JEAN-PAUL: You do? My, my, my. When I was your age I knew so little.

JEAN-PAUL (48): He might have come anyway. Besides, what difference does it make? Human life begins on the far side of despair, and who is to say whether despair is the cause or that despair is the effect. One thing happens and then another. Or you have cause and effect. For now, one is as good as another.

JEAN-PAUL (58): Well, it might matter whether we are conscious of it or not. Consciousness is the ultimate test - to be aware of what we are or are not.

JEAN-PAUL: I do not wish to discuss it with you. I've been over that ground. And I've been over it again. I can discuss it with other minds, but not your minds. You cannot lead me into any new directions. You will merely pull me back to where I've been.

JEAN-PAUL (38): And so how do you wish to pass the time? What do you wish to talk about?

JEAN-PAUL (48): Talk. Talk. While the crab above us pinches us in half. Cancer in the liver and the lungs.

JEAN-PAUL (18): Let's talk about Simone.

JEAN-PAUL: (Slowly, with great emphasis.) No. Not Simone.

JEAN-PAUL (28): Careful, old man. You'll bring another attack upon yourself. (The sound outside the great doors is of tanks rumbling through the streets and police dogs barking.)

JEAN-PAUL (58): Everyone calm down....Now would anyone like

152

to hear about my trip to Cuba, my impressions of Castro as a world leader?

JEAN-PAUL (38): Who is Castro?

JEAN-PAUL (58): No, let's not go through this again. Wars, Castro. We can't possibly have the same knowledge; do let's listen and learn from each other.

JEAN-PAUL: I told you I don't want to listen.

JEAN-PAL (28): Then what's the purpose of us being here?

JEAN-PAUL (38): Purpose! The most pathetic of human impulses is a yearning for purpose.

JEAN-PAUL (18): You're here to eat, dine, and to drink. What else do people do at a banquet?

JEAN-PAUL: Don't you understand? I know all about it. You open your mouths and I want to cry out against everything you say, but I won't get caught up in that trap. You aren't others.

JEAN-PAUL (48): We may forget sometimes, but we often have an inkling of understanding. But what can we talk with you about? Art? Music? Painting? Philosophy? Simone? Anything at all?

JEAN-PAUL (8): I want to hear about Castro.

JEAN-PAUL (58): I've been trying to tell you that in Cuba, the farmers are much better off under the Castro regime than under any other previous government. That's because Castro is a more thoroughgoing Marxist than many of his Soviet counterparts.

JEAN-PAUL: That was before Hungary! Don't talk to me of Marxism unless you are willing to remember Hungary!

JEAN-PAUL (58): Bah, you're asking us for the impossible, to remember what comes after us.

JEAN-PAUL (48): Whether it happens before or after us, it is history, and since Marxism provides the only valid interpretation of history, we learn the inevitability of certain historical processes. Hence we should be able to write a history of the future.

JEAN-PAUL (18): If it must happen so that your history of the future can be written, then where does my freedom come into play? My freedom to change the course of history, as it were?

JEAN-PAUL (48): From Marxism, if you pay attention, one can learn everything.

JEAN-PAUL (58): Such as we learn from Castro.

JEAN-PAUL (28): But this under the sign of Cancer is the outcome?

JEAN-PAUL (18): Whether we choose it or not?

JEAN-PAUL (38): You're beginning to sound like my friend Camus. There is only one philosophical question, and that is to live or die.

JEAN-PAUL: He is not our friend.

JEAN-PAUL (48): No?

JEAN-PAUL (58): No, I told him. I said that he wasn't revolting against Communism so much, but that he was revolting against himself.

JEAN-PAUL (28): What's freedom for but to revolt against one's self, one's very being?

JEAN-PAUL (48): As a good Marxist, you are free to be conscious of the inevitable.

JEAN-PAUL: Marxism teaches us nothing. It leads you out into the water and leaves you there, stranded, as the water rises over your head. You cannot know how you Marxists let the men of Hungary drown. You thoroughgoing Marxists did that. You gunned men down in the streets. If you knew that, you would change your minds. All of you.

JEAN-PAUL (48): How Fascist can you get, saying if you only knew what I know, you would change your minds! It is like a general leading his men to disaster. Don't think about the commands. If you only knew what I know, then you would do what I do now.

JEAN-PAUL: (*Ironically.*) When Hemingway met me in Paris,

154

there he was, standing there in his pajamas, wearing a green eyeshade around his head, like he had played poker in his sleep, and he grabbed hold of me and hugged me in a great bear hug, and he said that I was a general. I'm only a captain, he said, but you are a general.

JEAN-PAUL (48): But this time a Fascist general.

JEAN-PAUL: That' why there is no conversation possible between us. You *would be* me if you knew what I know. I cast you all off long ago. Your mannerisms, your affectations, your philosophical blunders, your romantic idealisms.

JEAN-PAUL (38): Idealism is at the very heart of cynicism, isn't it?

JEAN-PAUL: What am I supposed to do? Sit here forever and listen to you tell me stories that I already know? Listen to arguments that I've outgrown? I choose not to be surrounded by your faults, that's why I threw them off. I refuse to be bored out of my mind by all of you. I see through you.

JEAN-PAUL (18): If you refuse, then prove yourself as a general. Revolt against yourself. Revolt against Roquet's torture. When one is caught between the insufferable and the intolerable, there is nothing to do but revolt.

JEAN-PAUL: What should I do? Try to murder Roquet with my bare hands?

JEAN-PAUL (18): Why not?

JEAN-PAUL (8): In my story, the knight kills the devil.

JEAN-PAUL: And becomes a hero. I've lived long enough to see the death of heroism. Jean, I am no knight.

JEAN-PAUL (18): Well, if you are not man enough to do it, I will. I'll keep Roquet out. I'll prove my freedom to you.

JEAN-PAUL: The greatest freedom is not to have to prove you're free.

JEAN-PAUL (18): *(He stares intently at the old man and then picks up the coat stand and places it across the two doors, so the doors can no longer be opened.)* There, and I'll show you what I think of Maxim's food.

(He starts knocking platters of food to the floor and overturning the place settings. Young JEAN'S story scatters every which way.)

JEAN-PAUL (8): My story! You're losing my story!

JEAN-PAUL (18): I'm sorry, Jean-Paul. *(He helps Young JEAN gather up the pages of The Transcendental Knight.)* I'll help you gather the pages.

JEAN-PAUL: Now, you see what you've done. You've made a mess of everything.

JEAN-PAUL (18): Everything I say or do, you throw back in my teeth.

JEAN-PAUL: Should I feast on your thoughts and grow fat?

JEAN-PAUL (18): I suppose the vision that you have is that we should all sit here and be lectured by you. You, with all your knowledge of what is to become of us, and we sit at your feet like poor dumb angels...

JEAN-PAUL: We have fallen like an angel, but we are not one.

JEAN-PAUL (18): All right then, like dogs at your feet, or like silly geese while you fatten up our livers with *your* wisdom, *your* experiences, *your* fascinating repertoire of anecdotes, *your* philosophical turns, as if you were Moses himself handing down the Ten Commandments, so that we cannot even be ourselves with you, because you will always be flaunting what we will become in our faces. You show me all the knowledge that I will eventually grow into, will age into, until I look exactly like you, talk the way you do, think like you...

JEAN-PAUL: I'm afraid it is inevitable, but to hear you carry on like this to see you scatter the table every which way, it only causes me great pain. I should have been better than that.

JEAN-PAUL (18): Don't talk to me of should, should all the time. You've forgotten what it's like to be young and to have the whole world exist as an infinite possibility. For me and young Jean, and for everyone else here, it's infinite. But for you it's finite. All over and done.

156

JEAN-PAUL: But I am what you will choose to be. Is that infinite?

JEAN-PAUL (28): You're not the only person locked inside of this room, Jean-Paul.

JEAN-PAUL: That's funny, but I would have said exactly the opposite. Roquet's amusement is that you are all telling me jokes to which I know the punch-line. And the jokes are long-winded and not amusing, and I know the outcomes.

JEAN-PAUL (48): Then regard us as others and save yourself.

JEAN-PAUL: I can't. It's impossible.

JEAN-PAUL (28): Why not? *(Outside the great doors, now barred by the coat stand, there are the sounds of a traffic jam.)*

JEAN-PAUL: I look at the door and say I am not a door. I look at the world and I say I am not the world. I affirm by negating all that is not me. How can I say to you you are not me? If you were someone else, I could kill you. But how can I kill you?

JEAN-PAUL (18): Try. Surely there must be enough knives around here.

JEAN-PAUL (58): This is ridiculous. Soon we'll all be at each other's throats. You feel superior to me. I feel superior to *(indicating JEAN-PAUL (48).)* him. It will soon boil down to big fish eat little fish, until we get down to little Jean.

JEAN-PAUL (8): I'm not little. I can take care of myself.

JEAN-PAUL (58): Quite right. We're the little ones. *(Indicating JEAN-PAUL.)* He's bitter because he has made all his choices.

JEAN-PAUL: Now you're even trying to turn young Jean against me.

JEAN-PAUL (58): Nobody's trying to turn anybody against you.

JEAN-PAUL: You're merely Roquet's tools. You're his rack, his whip, his spikes through the throat. You are strings in his fingers and he plays you like a harp.

JEAN-PAUL (28): Kill him then.

JEAN-PAUL: It's what he wants me to do. To try and kill him and prove my impotence against him.

JEAN-PAUL (18): You're afraid of him.

JEAN-PAUL: What more is there to be afraid of? I can hold out against him, if you be quiet....

JEAN-PAUL (58): It is not our words alone. It is our very presences.

JEAN-PAUL: Silence. Let's have silence. Silence won't hurt anybody. *(Silence, just long enough to make the audience uncomfortable, but not too long. Footsteps can be heard off in the distance. MAXIM'S voice going through the checklist for another banquet. A few lights go off in the chandelier. The only other sound is the squeak of young JEAN-PAUL'S pen as he continues his story.)*

JEAN-PAUL: With the lights so erratically, young Jean will find it difficult to complete his story....

JEAN-PAUL (48): Tell me, did I complete my quartet of novels?

JEAN-PAUL: Why do you wish to know?

JEAN-PAUL (48): *(Quietly but with feeling.)* Tell me. I want to know.

JEAN-PAUL: If I tell you, I will only destroy you.

JEAN-PAUL (48): That means I didn't? Or that I did and then they were hideous failures?

JEAN-PAUL: No, it means either. It simply means you are what you are up to a certain moment because of your ignorance. Should you know more, you become someone else. Another Jean-Paul, but not the one you are now. If you keep piling answer onto question after question, then eventually you become me, and look where I am. I am in the position of the tortured and the torturer, so save yourselves.

JEAN-PAUL (48): Save ourselves! What an ugly joke. *(To JEAN-PAUL (58).)* You can tell me things. You can tell me what happened afterwards.

JEAN-PAUL (28): Tell us about Simone. What happens to me and Simone?

JEAN-PAUL (18): *(Putting his hands over his ears.)* No, I don't want to hear about it. *(There is a rattling at the big doors, but they are not opened. They cannot be opened.)*

JEAN-PAUL (38): *(Pointing to JEAN-PAUL.)* Just look at his eyes. Can't you see everything about us there?

JEAN-PAUL (48): Sadists! You are all a bunch of sadists. *(ANTOINE ROQUET enters through the audience. He is followed by two WAITERS, MATHIEU and BRUNET, who carry silver trays and buckets of champagne....)*

ROQUET: Gentlemen, gentlemen, what's going on here? You've made such a mess of things. And our guest was so worried about looking great. And Maxim! Oh, my darling, he's going to be furious. He spent so much time on the food, trying to prepare something to make you happy.

JEAN-PAUL (58): What do we need food for?

ROQUET: Need? We supply the food, you supply the appetites. *(Going to the doors and removing the coat stand while the WAITERS clean up the tables. ROQUET indicates the coat stand.)* Now what is this doing here? You didn't think you could keep me out, did you? Is this how the modern guest treats his host? Really, Jean-Paul, I am greatly appalled. I really did expect much better table manners.

JEAN-PAUL (18): I was only trying to prove a point to this old man.

ROQUET: Quod Praemium tibi dedit? What reward did he give you? Oh really, my Latin is getting much better.

JEAN-PAUL: I am sure that it will be a comfort to you in your old age.

ROQUET: I do age well, don't I? And oh, Jean-Paul, you'll be happy to know that we finally found the violinist. He's a little late, but better late than never, right? Besides, you were getting on so well with your guests that you wouldn't have paid any attention to the music. But he really is a good one. One of the best. We get only the best here. The daring, adventurous ones. Ones who need to prove their freedom. But you don't, do you, Jean-Paul?

JEAN-PAUL: *(Pauses.)* Then send him in. *(From off-stage, we hear the sound of a violinist tuning up.)*

JEAN-PAUL (58): Does he know "one of These Days?"

ROQUET: You really didn't answer my question, Jean-Paul.

JEAN-PAUL: I would rather you send the violinist in.

ROQUET: Oh, no, there must be a slight misunderstanding. The only person allowed in this room from this moment on are you and your guests and perhaps a few more guests.

JEAN-PAUL: You lied before. I see no need to believe you now.

ROQUET: Dum vita est, spes est, eh?

JEAN-PAUL: Why not simply put me in a hall of mirrors?

ROQUET: I'm sure that even you realize that it is not the same thing. We even thought of cloning, you know - endlessly making duplicates of the same person - perhaps fill the room with hundreds of Jean-Pauls the way you are now, but we tried it on one person, and he absolutely adored it. Loved himself from beginning to end. Most probably he was an actor. So then I hit upon this scheme, and it's been so much more successful.

JEAN-PAUL (58): You said there might be more guests?

ROQUET: Perhaps.

JEAN-PAUL: Then these aren't all. I thought not. I expect others.

ROQUET: Others? Surely you must realize there can be thousands and send a new one in to upset your calm. A Jean-Paul at age thirteen might be a welcome addition to this company, don't you think? *(Heavy sarcasm.)* Oh he is such a darling, you will positively adore him. Or a Jean-Paul at fifty-two, or sixteen, even.

JEAN-PAUL: I hate them all.

ROQUET: Oh don't say that, Jean-Paul. One should keep an

open mind about these things. After all, they will all be here eventually.

JEAN-PAUL (38): There's not much room here.

ROQUET: Then we'll move the banquet to a larger room. That's logical enough, isn't it?

JEAN-PAUL: I didn't expect such a logical plan from you.

ROQUET: Of course not. You wanted things haphazard and unexplainable, but you forgot that the most absurd and unexplainable of all circumstances is a well-planned, logical situation. What can be more absurd?

JEAN-PAUL: You're playing with words.

ROQUET: Why not? I invented them, didn't I? Mathieu, get number twenty-one. Twenty-one is next.

JEAN-PAUL: Couldn't we have some other people in here?

ROQUET: No, I'm afraid not. You see all the invitations have been sent out. *(A boy of thirteen enters the room, carrying his cap in his hands.)*

JEAN-PAUL (13): Pardon me, monsieur, but is this the place where the banquet is being held?

ROQUET: Are you Jean-Paul?

JEAN-PAUL (13): Yes, sir.

ROQUET: And when were you born?

JEAN-PAUL (13): June 21, 1905.

ROQUET: *(Mock surprise.)* Oh, a Cancer. I just adore Cancers. They are so tenacious. Claws for hanging on. And your parents?

JEAN-PAUL (13): My father is dead.

JEAN-PAUL: You aspire to be God, Roquet.

ROQUET: How dare you. I simply wish to do my job so well that God aspires to be me....*(To JEAN-PAUL (13).)* And how is your Uncle Charles?

JEAN-PAUL (13): He is very fine. Do you know him?

ROQUET: Oh, a passing acquaintance. Well, come right in. We have a coat stand for your coat and your cap. I'm sure the guest of honor will make you welcome, won't you, Jean-Paul?

JEAN-PAUL: *(Weakly, very tired.)* Why of course....

ROQUET: Of course...Now if there is any number I can suggest to the violinist....*(Starts his exit toward the huge doors. The WAITERS go into the audience.)* It would be much easier if number twenty-one come forward. *(To JEAN-PAUL.)* He's really quite good on love songs, songs that go "Love, love, love, love." Ha-ha. *(Laughs ironically.)* But I'm sure you know that already....*(ROQUET slams the door, echoes of other doors can be heard. Another door, and then the violinist launching into a maudlin, sentimental love song. The lights in the chandelier go out.)*

THE END

Louis Phillips' most recent books are: THE WOMAN WHO WROTE KING LEAR and other stories (Pleasure Boat Studio), THE KILROY SONATA (a poetic sequence) and ROBOT 9 IN WONDERLAND (World Audience Publishers), and FIREWORKS WITH SOME PARTICULAR (stories, poems, plays, & humor pieces, published by Fort Schuyler Press).

Made in the USA
Monee, IL
07 July 2026

56544850R00095